...ve Moran has long been a passionate advocate for improving ...the senior living industry addresses the needs of older ...s and their families. This book is further evidence of ...ve's commitment to helping us get it right.

Dan Hutson
Senior Living Strategist, Innovator, Marketer

The right book at exactly the right time. Great employee culture IS the key to delivering great experiences. Steve gives us some great 'best practice' we can all learn from.

Kris Engskov
President of Aegis Senior Living

Every senior living leader who is serious about their culture needs to read this book.

Faith Ott
Founder of Sage Age Strategies

As he always does, Steve says what needs to be said, in a blunt, straightforward way. As it always is, it can be uncomfortable to read. If we put aside our sometimes hurt feelings and defensiveness and listen, we can see a path to a bright future written by someone with a deep love for our field, and a deep respect for those who do the work.

John Cochrane
President and CEO of HumanGood

Steve asked me to write a review, but honestly I really didn't want to because I've been so busy. But I respect him and wanted to be supportive. I began reading the first chapter just to be able to write something, and 60 minutes later I was still reading.

David Freshwater
Watermark Group

Finally! A leadership book that focuses on the senior li
industry. Steve provides fabulous life stories that are re'
to helping others become better leaders. If you are a cu
learning leader, this is a must-read!

Lori Alford
Co-Founder and
Chief Operating Officer of Avanti Senior Living

A wonderful book on culture that helps leaders to close the gap
between knowing what to do and actually doing it.

Michael Owens
Co-Founder of Influence Group

It's about time someone wrote a book like this, something for
senior living leaders to devour and live by.

Jacquelyn Kung
Founder of Senior Care at Activated Insights,
A Great Place to Work Company

This is a must-read book for those who want to enhance the
quality of their company's operating culture and performance.

Mel Gamzon
Principal of Senior Housing Global Advisors

As always, Steve brings us unique perspective as a thought
leader and 'would-be-consumer' of our necessarily evolving
programs and communities. In his manner and his writing,
Steve demands that we think and go beyond our 'comfort zones'
in order that we as a sector, and the folks whom we ultimately
serve, can thrive and find joy... this book contains a series of
insights and constant reminders of what's most important in
doing our best work together.

Sean Kelly
President and CEO of The Kendal Corporation

Leaders are not born, they are nurtured. Steve's book is a clear road map showing you how to become a true leader with heart and soul.

Gene Guarino
President of RAL Academy

LEAD, DON'T MANAGE

LEAD, DON'T MANAGE

BY STEVE MORAN

For general information about our products or services, please visit our website, www.seniorlivingforesight.net, or contact us at smoran@seniorlivingforesight.net.

Library of Congress Cataloging-in-Publication Data is on file with the publisher.

Publishers Cataloging-in-Publication Data

Lead, Don't Manage; by Steve Moran

124 pages cm.

ISBN: 978-1-7346864-0-1 Paperback
978-1-7346864-1-8 ePub
978-1-7346864-2-5 Mobi

Printed in the United States of America

Dedication

This book is dedicated to my wife, Pat, and my kids, Steven, Paul, and Rebecca, who have traveled so much life with me.

Creating a Place Where People Love Coming to Work Everyday

Table of Contents

Tenacious, Uncompromising and Honest

When I think of Steve Moran, these are the words that come to mind. He is tenacious in improving everything he touches. Whether it's the entire industry or an individual's life. It doesn't matter to him. He really does care! It's part of the reason I wanted to help him publish this book. The ideas and strategies he's uncovered through thousands of hours of research have to permeate senior living.

Steve's uncompromising commitment to telling the truth is what sets him apart. In fact, some of the truths in *Lead, Don't Manage*, might hurt your feelings, but that's okay. Steve's writing makes me a better leader and it will do the same for you. If you ever get a chance to meet him, you'll know he doesn't pull any punches. His honesty and straightforwardness are refreshing.

As you read, get your pen ready. You'll want to take notes!

—Dennis McIntee
Author, Speaker, Executive Coach at
Leadership Development Group

Foreword

As he describes in the book, Steve and I met for the first time under the most unusual of circumstances. I, mistaking him for a friend, walked up behind him at a conference, and slugged him hard in the arm. We've been sharing jabs—though verbally, not physically—ever since!

Some people see us as unlikely friends for a number of reasons, but we share a common vision that drives us and most of our conversations: to make senior living organizations better places to live and work. A lofty dream for sure! You've probably picked up his book because you're a dreamer like us. You know that senior living offers the most fulfilling work and is unmatched when it comes to the potential reward of supporting others. What other field allows you to build deep relationships that positively impact people's lives for weeks, months, and years?

At the same time, it's endlessly frustrating and at times maddening! Not all staff see the power their words and actions have on others, some people just seem to be in it for a paycheck, and fewer people seem interested in working in such a challenging field. That's where the book you are holding in your hands comes in.

Known for his ability to push buttons, rock the boat, and challenge the status quo, Steve is about to provoke you to think differently. A voracious reader and insatiable conversationalist, in this book he shares his gathered knowledge with you through engaging stories and reflective questions. His aim? To help you be a better leader.

As Steve shares, most relationships in business tend to be transactional, not relational. I hope that this book pushes you to focus on the latter, and that you won't just buy it and read it, merely thinking about it as a transaction to be completed. But that instead, you will buy it, read it, and think about how the lessons might apply to you and your team. Deepen the relationship with yourself as you reflect on your leadership style, and deepen the relationships with those who surround you as a leader.

Senior living CAN be a better place to live and work! And when it is, all of us dreamers will triumph!

—Denise Boudreau-Scott
Drive

Introduction

Over the last eighteen months, I have spent a huge amount of time thinking about the senior living workplace culture. There are some really great cultures, some so-so cultures and frankly, some pretty terrible cultures.

This book is not for leaders/managers of terrible cultures. They won't read this book. They will see it as a waste of time and energy. They will think I am naive or that I don't understand the challenges of owning and operating a senior living organization. They will believe I don't really understand how hard it is to hire, motivate, and keep any employees, let alone good ones. They don't even think or wish it could get better. All they hope for is that market conditions will turn around, or that the coming age-wave will give them huge profits.

In good economic times, they may perform well financially, which means their bosses or stakeholders will like them. But the people who work for them know they are not leaders at all, rather they are managers. Some managers are pretty good, and some—most—are really *not* that good.

For You...

This book is for those of you who have great cultures and are great leaders, but still struggle with creating the culture you desire. For you, my biggest worry is that the struggle will make you want to give up... that you will believe that Starbucks, Zappos, In-N-Out Burger, Chick-fil-A, Google, and Facebook can create great cultures and have more amazing applicants than they can handle, even when unemployment rates are breathtakingly low, but that you can't.

"Everyone needs a leader, and everyone can become a better leader. Becoming a better leader is our honor and our obligation if we are fortunate enough to have a team that we are responsible for. Thank you, Steve, for caring enough to share with us all a better way to become great leaders."

—Gene Guarino,
President of RAL Academy

I have faith that you can do it, and this book is a tool to help you make that happen. It is *hard*—mind-numbing, I-want-to-give-up-or-shoot-myself hard. You will do the things in this book, and employees will still do stupid, scary things. They will quit on you and they will say bad things about you.

You will have an internal dialog where you tell yourself it would be a whole lot easier to write a bunch of policies and procedures than to hold people's feet to the fire, punish them, or fire them if they break the rules. You will tell yourself that you will not risk having your feelings hurt or feeling stupid. You will find yourself thinking you did all you could and it still went very wrong and you got screwed by a team member. This will be followed by an internal guilt trip where you think about all the little things you could have done differently that might have given you a different, better outcome.

I know this because as I am writing this I am just coming off of one of those experiences, and it was really terrible. I found myself thinking it would have been a lot easier if I just didn't care. I can list twenty little things I wish I had done better.

It is my heart that is really hurting, doing the talking. My rational brain tells me even if I had done all "those things" better, it would have still ended badly. This is true for you, too. We are human; we never do everything perfectly. But when a team member wants to betray you, to hate you, to hurt you, there is nothing you can do to stop it.

You are an amazing leader who wants to get better, or you would not be reading this. Know that I have absolute faith that you can create a culture that is better, more attractive than Starbucks, Zappos, In-N-Out Burger, Chick-fil-A, Google, or Facebook, and that you can have people begging to work for your organization.

What senior living organizations do is holy work: supporting residents living out the last chapters of their lives, and family members who are walking that journey with their older loved ones. But it gets better; senior living is providing opportunity that exists nowhere else for individuals who are working at the bottom of the employment stack—who in many cases would be economically better off not working and just collecting public benefits—to be whatever they want to be.

As a leader in senior living, you have the opportunity to be their guide, to change lives, and to make the world a better place in profound ways.

This book is about helping you get even better than you already are.

Acknowledgments

Creating acknowledgments for a book is something that is fraught with danger. I know I will unintentionally leave out someone who should be mentioned, but here it goes.

Each of my friends and colleagues who provided a block quote or a book endorsement: you took the time to help me when you didn't have to.

My wife, who this first book is dedicated to.

There are a few senior living leaders who won't even know they are being named, but they befriended me when no one had ever heard of Senior Living Foresight or Steve Moran. Their willingness to let me interview them and to encourage me—when I was just some off-the-wall guy writing risky stuff—really kept me going. This includes Loren Shook, Paul Mullin, Stephanie Handelson, Shannon Ingram, the amazing Granger Cobb, David Freshwater, Larry Cohen, Tom Grape, and Faith Ott—my very first Senior Living Foresight sponsor.

Julie Davis, the amazing vice president of communications at Brookdale—who still scares me to death, and who I suspect I annoy more than just about any writer—but has taught me more than she will ever know.

The whole Senior Living Foresight Team: Pam McDonald, podcaster extraordinaire; Sue Saldibar, who is a monster when it comes to writing; Wendy D'Alessandro, a writer and social media wiz; Rebecca Wiessmann, who keeps all the wheels turning and organized for me to mess up again; Fara Gold, who has pushed us to grow faster and smarter; Elizabeth George, our newest writer; Kent Mulkey, who is my brother-from-another-mother; and the wisest of the wise, Jack Cumming. A special thanks to Kandi Short who recently exited.

To Dennis McIntee, who convinced me I could do this and helped me figure it all out.

Finally, to those of you who read Senior Living Foresight, who tell us your stories, who call us out when you disagree.

And a final apology for those of you whom I left out. Because I didn't leave you out on purpose, and I don't want to leave you out, you can add your name below.

And the biggest thanks of all to:

Chapter 1

When They Kick You in the Teeth

This may seem like a weird topic to start off this book. It is the last chapter I wrote and it may actually be the most important chapter in the book.

The consistent underlying message in *Lead, Don't Manage* is that in order to have a great organization you must develop deep, meaningful relationships with your team members. This means investing time in those relationships and being vulnerable. What is odd about the ideas in this book is that they are insanely simple to understand and at the same time insanely hard to get right—and they are always a work in progress.

My biggest fear for you is that you will read this book, try some things, and give up when they won't work very well at first. My second biggest fear is that you will start building relationships with some team members and it will go super well... at first. Then just when you think, "That book Steve Moran wrote is amazing. I am becoming the leader everyone wants to follow," things will completely blow up.

A team member will take your friendship, your transparency, your vulnerability, and turn against you. Then, because you developed this great relationship with them it will hurt more than usual, it will make you want to cry, and really piss you off. If you are anything like me, here's what will happen.

At first you will experience a feeling of disbelief. You will wonder if that person you thought was your friend, as well as a team member, is playing some sort of bad, gone-wrong practical joke on you. You will slowly come to understand that the attack is real and deep and meant to be hurtful.

Next you will start to wonder if you actually did something wrong. You will replay in your head every interaction you had with that person. You will be baffled by the hurt they are causing in response to your kindness. You will start to identify things you could have possibly said or done better. And trust me, you will be able to identify some of those things, and you will wonder.

But here is the thing: we are never perfect, we never get anything 100 percent right. We could always do something a little better. We could say more, or say less. We could provide one more opportunity or accommodation.

When this happens, and I promise it will, the danger is that you will revert back to your old ways. You will think, "Forget this relationship thing, it's not worth it." That it creates too many negative emotions, anger, sadness, and resentment.

There is no doubt that not building relationships beyond the basic level of what is needed for them to exist makes it much easier to avoid these situations. It also makes it easier to fire someone. Firing someone is never easy, but when you have to fire someone who is your friend... it's *terrible*.

> Remember the old British quote, that only dead fish swim with the stream.
>
> —Jacquelyn Kung,
> CEO, Senior Care Group

Been There Done That

This has been a theoretical concept to me until a few weeks ago, which I suppose is why I neglected to write this chapter sooner. Then out of the blue I received an email saying that an expense reimbursement I sent had never been received, along with an accusation that I deliberately chose not to pay the bill, money I owed legally and morally, because I was about ready to fire them. Or alternatively, that I was struggling with my cash flow and had delayed payment. These allegations were made in spite of a five-year history of paying on time or early, and in spite of providing significant sums of extra cash wired the same day they were requested in order to prevent impending doom in the form of car repossessions and disconnected cell phones.

It was simply a lost check, that as soon as I figured out was lost, I covered with a wire transfer, that still took a few days to work through the system and included a significant overage to cover overdraft fees. Yet instead of any sense of belief it was followed by a series of emails saying, "I quit, you dirty bastard" (not quite those words, but that attitude). That outlined a long list of slights, towards him and his family. Some big and some trivial.

This was someone I had a decades-long history with, someone who has on numerous occasions turned to me for help in times of crisis—emotional and economic. I have always been there for him to the maximum of my capacity, without judgement and without restraint.

The emails not only tarnished my reputation, but my whole family's. We were accused of emotionally taking advantage of him and his family, of lying, of breaking promises, and of not demonstrating the right amount of love and respect.

In his mind I am sure he believed all of these things to be true. I am willing to admit that my beliefs are not accurate either, but he directly accused me of being deliberately abusive and mean. While I could have done things a bit differently, nothing I did was ever with malicious intent. I was practicing—to the best of my ability—everything I have written about in this book.

Even now, there is a thought running through my head that says, *Don't ever get that close to any of your team members again. It is not worth it.* And yet, I refuse to give in to that temptation. It is akin to saying I am never going to have another romantic relationship, because the breakup hurt too much.

It is worth it, even when you get kicked in the teeth.

Chapter 2

Strong Relationships— Friends Not Just Coworkers

The single biggest factor that will determine how successful you are as a leader is the quality of the relationships you have with your individual team members. Being a senior living leader is one of the most amazing jobs in the whole world—if you value relationships.

It is hell if you are not much of a people person. At an intimate gathering of senior living leaders I proposed that creating and reinforcing culture was the most important job a CEO has. I was shocked when I got pushback that included a long list of other things people felt the CEO was responsible for. The list was accurate for sure, but it did nothing to change my belief that culture is the number one priority, and not by a little bit. This is no less true for regional managers, executive directors, and department heads.

Yes, leaders have budgets, regulations, scheduling, and dozens of other things that require their attention. But at the end of the day every leader is the conductor of an orchestra; the goal is to make heavenly music by directing the instruments that are your team members. Individually, these people might seem ordinary or even unpleasant. But by blending their unique skills, talents, and quirks in just the right way, the result is a magical, majestic concert. A concert that is only magical because you, as the conductor, bring out the best in each individual.

The key to making this magical music is the relationship you as a leader have with your team, and the relationship your team has with their team, and the relationship those people have with their teams and each other, all the way down to the front-line staff.

> We spend more time with our colleagues than our spouses. Why not be friends, IF we can earn the respect and serve our team's needs in a fair way?
>
> —Jacquelyn Kung,
> CEO, Senior Care Group

This starts by seeing your direct reports as friends and not just employees, team members, or underlings. I get that as the CEO or regional—and perhaps even as an executive director—it is impossible or unlikely that you can be friends with everyone in your organization, though you can be friendly with all of them. But it is critical that you are friends with those who report directly to you (the part you have control over). It is also ideal that you are friends with the person you report to, though you have limited control over that relationship.

The level of friendship will vary from individual to individual. Some will naturally be closer than others and that's okay, as long as you do not let the closest relationships cloud your judgment. While each situation and each relationship is different, it is rarely possible to have your best friend be a direct report.

You might be thinking, "Wait a minute, I have a couple of direct reports who are superstars at what they do. I don't like them or trust them much, but they get results." Trust me, this is not good enough. At some point it will come back to bite you in the ass.

> In my nearly 40 years in this industry, I have grown to realize that not only having a business relationship, but also knowing your team members personally, and truly being interested, has been tremendous in staff retention and building a strong culture!
> —Faith Ott,
> Founder and President of Sage Age Strategies

Strong relationships come from spending enough time with each of your direct reports to know what is important to them. I live this out in my own organization. I really want to understand what makes my direct reports tick. I want to know what they are passionate about, what their big dreams are, what they hate, and what they are afraid of. I want to know what their hobbies are, and about their kids and grandkids. I want to know their quirks. I want to know what their ambitions are. And I want them to know all that stuff about me as well.

This is critical to you as a leader and to your organization for two reasons. The first, though maybe the least important, is that it will make your job easier and more fun. The second is that a time will come when you need to have a hard conversation with a team member. If your relationship is strictly business when that happens, it can feel like a personal attack. Although you would never say, "You are not a good person," those are oftentimes the words people will hear. They will get defensive, problems won't get solved, and performance will slide. Suddenly, their day becomes about avoiding you, getting yelled at, getting in trouble, and losing their jobs rather than doing the job they're paid to do. They refuse to take risks that may be beneficial to your organization because they are so paralyzed by the fear of getting into trouble. People need to take those risks because organizations need new ideas.

Daniel Cable tells the story of research done by Jaak Panksepp, an Estonian neuroscientist, regarding rats and play:

> When two young rats were put together in a test environment they would almost always start playing; chasing each other, wrestling, and they actually make unique measurable chirps of joy when they are happy and excited.
>
> Then the researcher took a small tuft of cat fur and put it in their play space which, as you would expect, activated their fear mechanisms. The rats went from play to defense. Without the fur, the rats averaged 50 invitations to play over a 5 minute period of time. When the cat fur was put in the play area play invitations went to zero. At this point you are thinking so what? But here is what is really fascinating and super important. When the rat fur was removed it took 3 days for the rats to start playing at all. And even more sobering and

> disheartening: the rats level of play never returned to the pre-fur days.
>
> —Alive at Work: The Neuroscience of Helping Your People Love What They Do by Daniel M. Cable

This is particularly sobering because, while some employees are able to shake off a negative encounter with their boss, most can't. That means, after that negative encounter, their work performance and further interactions with you continue to be damaged.

If a team member is afraid and everything they do is from a defensive position, they are more likely to miss things and more likely to make mistakes. In senior living, those mistakes could cost someone their health or their life.

A friend of mine once had a great job as a regional director at a decidedly *mediocre* senior living organization in Illinois. She may not have been actively job hunting, but she kept her eyes open for the perfect new opportunity. It dropped into her lap: a job with a bigger organization, making more money, in an area where her spouse has family. She accepted the position and moved her family halfway across the country to start this dream job.

But when she got there she discovered that she had jumped from the frying pan into the fire. It was hell; the pressure on her was intense because owners and supervisors only seemed to care about the bottom line. They micromanaged everything she did, watching census numbers and sales funnels. Nothing was ever right and nothing was ever good enough. My friend, who is an incredible and competent leader, found herself going home at the end of the day stressed out and wiped out. That stress impacted her interactions with her husband and young children. She was worried about her job and she found herself living in a kind of alternate world where she felt attacked and defensive all the time.

In her role, she had to make and influence decisions that impacted thousands of lives. She directly oversaw the seniors who lived in the communities she was responsible for, the team members who provided care to those seniors, and the family members of the seniors and the team members. The pressure she was under meant she was not bringing her best to anyone—not the seniors, not their families, not the team members, and not her own family. The result: she started looking for a new job.

> Building trust with someone new takes time and effort. Once established, it becomes 'green fertile space' for two or more people to share ideas, to be creative, and to take risks without fear. Once trust is broken, it is hard to rebuild—nearly impossible to restore completely—on what has now become a foundation of doubt.
>
> —Lynne Katzmann,
> Founder and CEO of Juniper Communities

Relationships are essential because a strong team bond eliminates fear. If you are a "Yeah, this touchy-feely stuff is okay, but it only goes so far, what about the bottom line?" kind of person, have no fear: this is all about the bottom line. When you have good relationships, your organization will be more productive; if the team is happy and operating well together, your community will have higher occupancy, lower expenses, and a much better bottom line. If you have a great relationship with your team, your team will have a great relationship with residents and coworkers, and they'll be interested in furthering the mission of the team. That's going to make you more money. The bottom line is improved, recruitment is easier because they are telling their friends how much they love work, and it makes residents happier.

Allow me to give you a personal example that illustrates how important relationships are.

I fly twenty to thirty trips and eighty or ninety flight segments per year. My airline of choice is Delta. This means that, as a customer, I have a lot of interaction with Delta employees. My guess is that between the check-in counter, the boarding gate, and calls to reservations, I have at least three hundred interactions with them each year. That's… a lot. Each of those interactions provides an opportunity for me to have a great experience, a terrible experience, or an unmemorable experience.

The great interactions make me want to tell all my friends to fly Delta. The unmemorable experiences are fine; what needed to happen happened. Nothing wrong with that, in fact it's a lot better than terrible, but ultimately they don't particularly help me like Delta more. My brain says, "Yep, that is the way it is supposed to be."

The terrible interactions are the *worst*. Because of the way our brains work, those are often more memorable than the great ones. What fascinates me is that it only takes a tiny, tiny thing to either make a great experience or a terrible experience. I have thought a lot about the negative experiences, the super frustrating experiences, and they are usually the result of just one little trigger.

But what ends up happening is that the little trigger leads to a complaint. When it is handled right, they fix the problem or explain the circumstances and things are fine. Too often, though, the customer service person becomes defensive and their typical response is to treat me, the customer, like I am stupid and/or unreasonable. That, in turn, makes me resentful. I am resentful because what they are really saying to me is that they don't care about me as a person, they only care that I spend money with their company so they can have a job, and they want to be able to do that job without any disruption. The worst insult you can deliver to any individual is the message that they don't matter.

Here's a specific example: I typically fly out of Sacramento, California and, like most airline counters, there are two lines. The long line is for people who fly occasionally. The second, shorter line is for premium fliers, folks who fly a lot and are loyal to a single airline. I work hard to stay loyal to Delta and spend my money like a premium passenger. For me, this is about making flying less of an unpleasant experience or maybe even turning it from unpleasant to pleasant. Though, I confess that as I am writing this, it makes me sound a little bit like a snob but, dammit, I deserve a better experience if I'm willing to pay for it. The issue that arises in Sacramento is that they don't seem to have gotten the concept. They always have just one person working at the counter for the premium line but plenty of employees for the regular line. This means that I have, on more than one occasion, stood in the premium line feeling stupid and mad as I watch people, who arrived later than I did and got in the regular line, reach the counter first. I realize that you can't just keep moving the premiums to the front of the line because then there would be times when the non-premium line would never move. The way this problem is solved at most counters (except the Delta counter in Sacramento) is that the agents in the regular line alternate, taking a premium passenger every other person they serve.

It's a little thing, so I try to get to the airport early enough that I am not rushing to make it to the gate. But, as I stand there and time goes by and I'm looking at my watch and I'm seeing those non-premium passengers get their business taken care of faster, I get more and more ticked off. To the point where it drives me crazy.

One particular time I was running a little late and I could see the gate agents were clueless, not caring at all about the travel status of who was in line. The employees were just going through the motions and, by the time I finally get to the counter, I was in a full-blown, pissed off rage, even though I know it is a little stupid thing. I just had to say something, hoping that it will get them out of clueless mode… I thought, *Control yourself, Steve, be nice about this.* I complained and, while I was not a raging maniac, if you had watched you would have known I was upset. Feeding my anger were a number of other premium customers who were equally frustrated.

At this point the gate agents had two options. They could have said, "You're right, we really screwed this up. We were short-staffed and we stopped paying attention. We are sorry and will work at doing better next time." Instead, what they did say was, "We have too many customers and we have to help them in order as they get in line." While that wasn't a terrible response, they followed it up with something far worse: "How would you feel if you were stuck at this desk all day and people were yelling at you? There aren't enough of us here to help everyone." In effect, what they were saying to me was, "Screw you, I don't care about you as a premium customer, I don't care about you as a customer at all, I actually care more about me and my job and how much I hate my job, than I do about you."

In turn, I got even more upset and more angry. I vowed in my head to use my status to complain to everyone, to get these gate agents in trouble. Perhaps I should have been more sympathetic to their situation, except that I am the customer—a good customer.

If only they had paid a little bit of attention, looked at the line, and thought for just a moment. If early on someone had said, "Folks, we're sorry, we have this delay and so this is what we're doing to make it as less painful as possible. We know you're waiting and impatient and your time is valuable." If they had shown a little bit of empathy, I would have felt completely different. Everyone would have felt completely different. Instead of being mad we would have been sympathetic. But they didn't do that, they passed their unhappiness and dissatisfaction onto me, the customer.

The question is, how do we create work environments where our employees love coming to work? Delta is not taking good care of their employees. The company isn't providing enough staff, enough training, and isn't giving them enough love. Employees are frustrated with their job and their employer, and that poor working relationship feeds on grumbling in the break room and conversations that take place before and after work. The frustration trickles down and lands full force in how they treat customers, the people who ultimately provide the money that pays their wages.

These employees have no way of striking back at the CEO of Delta and, while they could potentially complain to their supervisor, that person likely doesn't have the power to fix the problem but does have the power to fire the complainer or make the life of the complainer miserable. The only way to get back at the company who is making them miserable is to not care about the customers. Or, if they are really angry with the company, treat customers badly. Rather than supporting the company they work for, they attack the company's bottom line.

We all want to feel special and cared for. Team members want to walk into work knowing that their coworkers are glad they are at work that day. They want to feel glad their coworkers are there, too. They want to know that their supervisor is glad to see them; that their CEO, whom they've never met, understands that they are an important part of the team. These positive relationships create a happiness that is passed down to the residents, to the customers, to everyone.

Unlike Delta, American, and United, Southwest Airlines has really figured this out. Even though Southwest has 58,000 employees, they understand the value of each individual in the organization. It trickles down from the top. Their founding CEO, Herb Kelleher, lived this out. He really cared that—until Southwest got to more than 1,000 employees—he knew the name of every single person.

I write a lot of articles on leadership and culture. I go to conferences with big name speakers who give talks on the subject and I read twenty or thirty books every year about the subject. I give a keynote titled "How to Be a Leader That Everybody Wants to Follow." In that presentation, I share the formula on how to do just that. Yet, if I'm brutally honest with myself, I am not sure that, in six months or a year, the people who attended my talk will be that type of leader.

It's not because they're bad people or that they don't know what the problem is. Rather it's that, while there is lots of data out there about what great leadership looks like and what great organizations look like, doing the work is really, really tough. It requires thinking about leadership differently and thinking about your team members differently. It requires doing things that don't seem very significant, very impactful, or very glamorous... things that don't seem very leader-like.

If you asked me about this a year ago, I probably would have told you the way I see the problem is that these leaders are not spending enough time thinking, reading, or attending conferences about leadership, but that is not it. In some ways, being a great leader and having a great culture is a lot like dieting: all you have to do to lose weight is to exercise more and eat less, with an emphasis on eating less. Easy, right? Except that it is actually super hard to do. We have a lifetime of habits and limited willpower. We have gotten used to doing things the way we do them. So the big challenge is this: how do I make radical changes in how I think about my culture and then translate that into new behaviors? Today I find myself thinking more in terms of "How do I help leaders close the gap between knowing what to do and actually doing it?"

But, maybe I'm wrong. Maybe, instead of talking about what it means to be a great leader, the more important question is: what does it mean to be led?

Ask yourself: How do I want to be led? How do the people who report to me want to be led? I am not sure we actually spend much time thinking about it from their perspective, but that is where the rubber really meets the road.

> There are so many things that have grabbed my attention, and that I've already implemented in my day-to-day interactions with our team. In particular, asking, "How do you want to be led?" What a great paradigm shift!
>
> —David Freshwater,
> Chairman of the Watermark Group

- I want to be led by somebody who inspires me, and who lets me know the work I'm doing is making a difference in the lives of my customers, in the lives of my coworkers, and in furthering the mission of the organization.
- I want a leader who helps me be more effective in reaching my goals, regardless of what the goals are. Or, in some cases, I need a leader who helps me figure out what my goals should be, what I am capable of.
- I want a leader who believes that I have the ability to reach those goals and who helps me believe that I can reach them. A leader who will buck me up when I am discouraged.

I've had a lot of leaders tell me that they'd be more effective if they just had better people to lead. It sounds reasonable but it is **dead** wrong! In truth, every leader in every organization in every industry says or thinks the same thing, which makes you realize that a good leader doesn't wait around for better people. People are pretty much all the same and they are as good or as bad as their leader makes them.

What too many leaders have failed to appreciate is that people want to be led in a positive direction. It's like this: if I'm a good leader, then my leadership goals are congruent with the individual goals of each team member. If one of them has a goal to be good at what they do, then I must be excited about them being good at what they do as well. If their goal is to eventually grow into my position as a leader, then I must be excited about them growing into my role or, in some cases, growing into an equivalent role in another organization. I should be doing all I reasonably can to assist them in getting there. If their goal is to use their current position as a stepping stone that will allow them to grow to the point that they will pivot out of that role and do something completely different, even in another industry, then that must be my goal as well.

When my goals are their goals, and their goals are my goals, they will be happier, work harder, and I will be happier and work harder. The existing organization will benefit overall. And, even though helping someone grow into their dream job may mean I will lose an amazing team member at some point, the work environment I have created will make recruiting a replacement a piece of cake.

Some pro tips: the person you are helping needs to be willing to do the hard work. You *also* need to be willing to help *everyone*, more or less equally, who is willing to do the hard work. This may mean finding additional mentors if there are too many team members for you to help by yourself. Finally, giving help is a great thing, an important thing, but if it becomes clear that the help you are giving is not appreciated or not working, then *you must stop.* Giving to someone who does not appreciate the help or takes advantage of it will destroy your soul. It will make you less likely to help the next person and it will keep you from doing the other important work you do.

Chapter 3

Meaningful Work

Every person wants to feel like the work they are doing is meaningful. In the senior living space, a big part of work involves personal care... things like clipping toenails, washing another person's armpits or genitalia, wiping adult bottoms, and changing adult diapers. To be completely frank, these tasks can be rather gross.

A caregiver who does this work may very well wonder, "Why am I doing this?" or "Why me?" The obvious reason is because the clients are dirty, which is unhealthy, and they need to be cleaned up but they can't do it themselves. To deal with this, a caregiver's internal narrative goes something like this: "Okay, it's gross but someone has to do it and I am getting paid to do it. I really need the money, so even though I hate what I am doing, it is better than not getting a paycheck." The problem is that the rest of the story too often goes like this: "I know the work needs to be done and I mostly like the people I care for, but my boss has no idea how bad it is, how gross it is, how hard it is. In fact, I am not sure my boss even knows my name or cares how good a job I do. All they really care about is their big fat bank account. The people who work at Starbucks or McDonald's don't have to put up with this and I bet that is a better job. When I get home I am going to apply there and quit this stinking job."

What is amazing is that it is possible for a leader (though, not a boss) to help caregivers change that narrative to something like this: "Yeah, this is kind of dirty and stinky and the mess is bad, but I am taking care of someone who used to be able to do this for themselves, and can't anymore. They probably hate this as much as I do. Once I am done cleaning them and helping them dress, they can go out and be productive, and have wonderful relationships with other residents and with their families. Because I am doing my job well, when the family visits they will have a great time with my resident friend. The other thing I like about doing this work is that if I didn't do it, one of my coworkers, who are my friends that I like and respect, will have to do it instead of me. They are already overburdened so I want to help lighten their load."

The narrative at the end of the day then becomes, "I am exhausted, I wiped eight butts today and that's eight lives that I made better today. I've given eight people a much better quality of life, and they were able to go out and read and eat and have meaningful interactions with people, and that's a wonderful thing. I have made the world a better place and I am a part of something much bigger than I am."

> Purpose is where our industry beats the Fortune 100 Best Companies to Work For, and why I love working in senior care so much.
>
> —Jacquelyn Kung,
> CEO, Senior Care Group

This should be easy in industries that care for vulnerable people like senior living and health care. Starbucks does it selling coffee and Zappos does it selling shoes. It astonishes me that WD-40, a company that sells oil in spray cans, does it. WD-40 has some of the highest employee engagement scores and lowest turnover rates in the country... and they sell oil.

We get to actually change people's lives in senior living, and our turnover numbers and engagement scores are not anywhere near those of a "oil in a spray can" company.

I don't care whether you're the CEO, regional supervisor, nurse, salesperson, cook, dishwasher, or a care aide who's wiping bottoms—everyone has parts of their job that are not fun. Sometimes they are simply tedious or boring and sometimes they are miserable. Sometimes it's paying bills, sometimes it's cleaning up messes on the floor. No one is exempt.

What keeps great passionate team members and leaders going, what fires them up and inspires them are the other things they do before and after doing the unpleasant stuff. Leaders must constantly remind their teams that the work they do is important and meaningful... that it matters. It is easy to forget this when doing those unpleasant tasks. When caregivers know that, after they finish giving a bath or wiping a butt, they are going to get to sit with that resident for a few minutes to talk and listen to stories, it makes it all worth it. Together, they will laugh or cry or smile and that's what makes the gross stuff worthwhile. Caregivers need to be reminded that doing the hard stuff makes the easy stuff possible. Finally, I need to add, this means the team member must have enough time to do the meaningful stuff as well as the hard stuff.

Great leaders set reasonable goals for their team and individual team members. Imagine your leader promises you a $50,000 bonus if you keep your community 100 percent full for a year. Yeah, that $50k sounds outstanding, but then you start thinking about it. They're asking for 100 percent, which means not a single vacant day in twelve months. You realize that things happen and that you are totally dependent on operations getting rooms turned when there is a move-out. As you keep thinking about it, it dawns on you that deaths and hospitalizations all too often seem to come in waves, and that it is an impossible goal.

What at first seemed like a motivating incentive on steroids turns into, "I am being manipulated and treated like I am not smart enough to figure out that it is a worthless proposition. It's actually worse than worthless. It is counterproductive. It makes me feel jerked around and devalued. Either I'll work less hard or start looking for a new position… or both."

Stretch goals can be extremely successful and, if they have big payoffs, they can and should be fairly tough to achieve. When leaders set reasonable goals, team members feel challenged and empowered. They know reaching their goal will be hard, really hard, but they also know they are capable of getting there. But stretch goals can never be impossible, or they will have the opposite effect. If they are team goals, it becomes a powerful way to create team cohesion.

Instead of creating arbitrary expectations, start by letting team members set their own goals. It empowers them and, if the organization is functioning well, they will likely set their own big, audacious—but reachable—goals.

This should be more than just a tactical process such as high occupancy or number of rooms cleaned. The big shift comes when you help your team members to dream big about their life goals, both personal and professional. You might be tempted to think life goals are not your responsibility as a leader, or even that talking about personal goals strays into dangerous legal/ethical territory, but it will be your big-win strategy.

That being said, you cannot, under any circumstances, "force" a team member to disclose or talk about those goals, and likewise you cannot judge their goals, because they belong to them and not to you. You will mostly find that people don't have big goals. This may be your best opportunity for making a positive impact on their life: by helping them to dream bigger and to see all that is possible in their life.

Imagine that you have a team member who says their dream is to run the Boston Marathon. It would be easy to argue that their specific goal is unrelated to work and outside the employment relationship. You could easily write it off. Or, you could provide them time off to train, become a sponsor, or even get your whole organization to be the support team. You could offer some of your airline miles to fly there, or connect them with someone else you know who has run the marathon.

Now you have relieved some of that team member's burden and helped them with a huge stretch goal. That will make them like you and the organization much more. In turn, they will work harder because they know you are supporting them not just at work but in life.

In training for a marathon they will gain skills that will help them be better at their "day job," in your organization. These skills can seem so hard to justify because, on the surface, it is difficult to measure the ROI, but over time the payoff will be huge.

It is actually better than that. Imagine if every team member in your organization had the kind of dedication and discipline it takes to run a marathon. There is no doubt they would approach working for you with that same level of commitment. It is likely they would inspire others in your organization to become more dedicated and disciplined.

Helping your team is simply the right thing to do. This is a kind of moral judgment and to be clear, if you don't do it, then you are doing the wrong thing and even a bad thing. Even if you just don't care and stay neutral, that is the wrong thing to do.

We are all human and on this planet together. If you're walking down the street, driving down the freeway, out in the park... do you want to be with people who are happy accomplishing what they want to, or do you want to be with a bunch of frustrated people?

I want to be valuable to somebody or something. Oscar Wilde said that it's worse to be ignored altogether than it is to be talked badly of. When somebody attacks me, I know I've impacted their life, even if it's in a negative way. What is worst of all is to be in a situation where you're there but you feel invisible. Telling *and showing* your team that they matter, not just to your organization but as people in the world, is the most important thing you can do.

Chapter 4

Be Transparent

I get that each of us has a need for—and an expectation of—some level of privacy. But great leaders of great organizations still make sure their team members know who they are. Your team needs to know your passions and strengths. You need to be talking about your weaknesses because, even if you don't talk about them, your team will know better than anyone else what your weaknesses are. Admitting to and talking about those weaknesses will make them like you more and build their trust.

Your team needs to get to know you and they need to get to know each other. There are some really cool ways you can make this happen. One of my favorites comes from Kim Scott in her book *Radical Candor*, where she suggests three separate conversations you as a leader should have with each of your direct reports. You should tell each other:

1. Your life stories
2. What everyone's big and little goals are
3. How the organization and the leader can help the team member achieve those life goals

I want to spend some time on just the first conversation.

Mostly, when we interact with team members, it is all about work. Talking about our personal lives is outside of the realm of comfort for most leaders which makes it difficult for leaders to discuss. But it doesn't have to be complicated. Go for a walk, get coffee, even have the conversation over lunch, but it must happen away from work. Carve out an hour for this.

Here is how it works for me: I begin with a single rule, "This is not about work." Then I ask, "Starting with kindergarten or the earliest point, how did you get to where you are today?" It then becomes a conversation between two people just getting to know each other. I have to be careful, because as the boss I am used to doing most of the talking and that's an instinct that leaders need to rein in. I might ask some questions of clarification but ultimately it is their story and not mine. I would caution you also that, while they can volunteer things outside of what you could ask in the scope of an employment relationship, you have to be a bit careful about not probing in areas that would cause discomfort or cause you legal problems.

> Ask a group of team members to get in groups of two or three, and then have them make a list of all the things they have in common.
>
> —Steve Moran

You may find they will say some things that go against your personal, political, or religious views, and you have to be prepared for that. Then, when they are done, you need to be willing and prepared to tell your own story about how you got to where you are. Your telling must be transparent, authentic, and meaningful. It should also relate to the story that you were told. Finding points of connection will create steel-strong bonds. It probably does not need to be said but you have to be smart about your transparency... all the details of your last three divorces, your two bankruptcies, or other personal information may not be what you would want to talk about, but maybe some of it is, because vulnerability matters. As long as you don't cross the creepy or TMI line, the more vulnerable you are, the more people will like you.

It may be helpful to start with a less-intense, less time-consuming exercise. Ask a group of team members to divide into smaller groups of two or three and then have them make a list of all the things they have in common. Make the exercise more interesting by asking them to find something weird or obscure they have in common. It turns out that when people discover things they have in common, especially when they are weird or uncommon, they tend to like each other more and they feel more of a connection. In my case...

- The fact that I am paired with someone who is male is not that interesting because it is so common as to mean nothing.
- When I am paired with someone who is bald, even though there are a lot of bald men out there, it makes me like that baldy better and them like me better.
- Even more interesting, if I am outside my home state and meet someone from my home state, we become instant best friends.

- Even better is if we grew up in the same town or went to the same school.
- Or, it could be we share the same hobbies, interests, or we both have moles on our left shoulder.

When I do this exercise with large groups, I give them five minutes to make as long a list as they can. I promise prizes for the group with the longest list and for the group with the most obscure or unique connection.

In the previous chapter, we talked about big goals, and how it is my goal as a leader to help my team know or figure out their life goals—not just their career goals. I want them to know that they can reach those goals. I want to know what people's big life goals are. I want to know, if my team member could be anything they wanted to, what would that be?

It could be something as big as becoming the CEO of my organization or another organization. It could be something short-term: they have a new baby or a young child and want to be home at five o'clock every day. Or, perhaps, that they have a spouse who is in school and they want to figure out how to make sure that their spouse succeeds at that so he or she can reach their dream. Or they're trying to get pregnant and IVF is very expensive. Or, they want to paint paintings… or make films… or get into photography. It might be something as simple as getting to the point where they can earn another $0.50 or $1.00 an hour. Maybe they want to go from being a line worker to a supervisor. It might also be that they just want more training so they can be the very best at what they are already doing.

It could be anything, big or small.

Once you start asking those questions and learning about your team members, then you start thinking about their goals and asking yourself, "How do I, as a leader in this organization and a leader for this person, actually help them reach their goal?" Sometimes, it's a little or even a lot scary. It also means I have to recognize that, once I help this person reach their goal, they may leave their position or the organization. Even scarier, they might become my boss.

For instance, in my organization, I'm experiencing a lot of growth. I mostly use contractors right now, but I need to hire a full-time employee in the next few months. That scares me to death. It means payroll and a very personal responsibility for that person's life.

But, as I thought about this process, I began to see what kind of person I need to hire: someone who is inexperienced, new to social media marketing or a new graduate who will need some training, and someone who will also be willing to do some administrative work. It also means they won't stay with me long-term. This person will likely work with my organization for eighteen to forty-eight months as a place to learn, grow, contribute, and get some great real-life experience before they eventually leave me. And, when they do, I will celebrate because I will know that I played a big part in helping them achieve their goals, both personally and professionally. This puts me in the position of being able to watch their career growth and think, "I knew them when... I gave that guy his first job and taught him all I could, and now look at him."

I am not perfect at this, but being helpful to others is a life goal. I frequently get to interview well-known people in and out of the senior living industry who are, frankly, way above my pay grade and I always end my conversation by asking if there is anything I can do for them. It seems improbable most of the time, but it keeps me in that mind-set. More importantly, it is my goal to ask that question to people I really can help—the people who, most likely, will never be able to reciprocate that help. I do this because it is the right thing to do and it keeps me in the proper mind-set. As a bonus, it makes me feel good! That's something I am convinced is hardwired into all of us... or at least it was when we were born.

Chapter 5

Feedback and Accountability

As a writer today, everything I write is published online. But, earlier in my life, I would occasionally write pieces that were published in print. I find online publishing to be a lot more satisfying, mostly due to my ego. The time between finishing an article and when it appears on the web is a matter of weeks, sometimes days or, occasionally, just hours. Additionally, having content published on the web makes getting feedback easy and practically instant.

I guess I am pretty much like everyone else. I love positive feedback and cringe at negative feedback. I have discovered that, much to my dismay, I am pretty thin-skinned when I get criticism from readers. If you give me fifty affirmations and one critical comment, I am completely obsessed by the single criticism.

Some people do just fine with criticism. The majority who don't tend to react in one of two ways. They become super defensive, which means they either justify the thing being criticized or attack, which could be out loud or in their head (depending on the power in the relationship). Or they are crushed beyond reason, as in "I must be a terrible person and terrible at what I do," or "I really hurt that person's feelings, they probably hate me now." I confess to being the kind of person who is crushed by criticism emotionally, even when I know it is completely illogical to feel that way.

There are some good reasons for feeling either angry or crushed. Most criticism is not delivered well, even when well-intentioned and, to be honest, it is rarely well-intentioned. On top of that, particularly when it comes from people who don't know you well, it is often wrong.

Because of all of this, something is often overlooked: we always learn more from our critics than we do from our fans. This is true even when the critic is way off base. Strong relationships are so important because they make getting and giving criticism much more valuable. I produce about ten articles per month at Senior Living Foresight and those articles are read by tens of thousands of people. We tackle some sticky issues that do not always have easy solutions attached to them, which makes them worth talking about. This means that, a few times a month, I get questions about my wisdom, sanity, and, occasionally, even my morality. Often they are thoughtful and turn into a productive dialogue but, other times, they are just mean, "gotcha" kinds of messages from someone who gets their kicks from being a troll. Yet, as weird as this sounds, even those messages hold some nuggets of truth or value. As a transparent leader, you must be willing to take all feedback, not just the positive feedback. Here's a personal example of transparency: one of my weaknesses is that I have too many important initiatives going on pretty much all the time. I know this is not great leadership from someone writing a leadership book, but I am hoping you will forgive me this for the moment. Because I always have so much going on, I occasionally miss things, let things slip through the cracks, or I say or do something that is suboptimal.

> I really respect the McKinsey way of giving feedback: agree on what you both observed happened, describe how it made you feel, and describe what you'd prefer to see next time, and why.
>
> —Jacquelyn Kung,
> CEO, Senior Care Group

A part of the human condition is that we are mostly terrible at self-monitoring. In many cases, we simply don't see that the stuff we are doing is wrong or hurtful and, of course, we don't see when we drop the ball. Conversely, we are often too hard on ourselves when we should be kinder and more forgiving. This is why feedback is so critical.

One of the core values/expectations of my publishing organization is that we hold each other accountable, starting with me. If I disappoint my team, or I screw something up, I expect them to tell me that. The goal is to do it with respect. Most of the time, they say, "Hey, there's this thing you promised to do, or you didn't do," and they are usually right about it. Maybe I got busy, or I forgot, or I was insensitive.

The only way to achieve that level of transparency is for the team to know each other really well and feel confident that we can trust each other. When mistakes happen, your team *knows*. They can tell when a mistake is simply a mistake. Your team will know you're willing to make amends and they can tell whether you're being genuine or just placating them. This then becomes an opportunity for you, as a leader, to make things better. A leader's willingness to be accountable, admit their mistakes, and apologize, is critical. You have to be willing to say what needs to be said. You have to admit your mistakes, say yes to new ideas, and say no to the ineffective ideas.

Chapter 6

You Don't Know It All

Do you like to be told what to do? Of course not! No one does, or at least *almost* no one. A point of clarification: being told what to do is not the same as teaching, which, when done well, is a joyous experience. I am also not talking about those rare moments when you need to issue a "Stop" command to prevent immediate harm. In both work and personal relationships telling people what to do strips them of autonomy. It says "I don't trust you, I don't trust your skills; I don't trust your judgement." Not giving your team members trust or autonomy is sort of like putting them in a box. It is saying, "I want you to do this thing, I want you to do it this way, and I don't care if you have a better idea or method. Do it my way, whether it's the right way or not."

How demoralizing is that? What if your employee has a better idea? Or what if they use a different method to achieve the same results? Giving people that autonomy is essentially saying, "I trust you."

Pam McDonald, who hosts the Senior Living Foresight podcast, writes occasional articles and does all the Senior Living Foresight copyediting. She and I have talked a lot about the need for autonomy and, specifically, her need for autonomy. In fact, one of the things I really admire in Pam is that she has made a personal decision not to work in environments where she can't have autonomy. One of the reasons she likes being part of the Senior Living Foresight team is that I say to her, "Pam, there is this thing I need to get done. Can you do it?" If she is able to, I say, "Awesome, have at it." She knows I trust her to get things done and, if she needs help, she'll come to me for answers or guidance. As leaders, we want people to do things the same way we do things. Likely that is because we think it's the best way to do things, but mostly we want them to do things our way because it makes us comfortable. As an important side note, I do try to limit my requests to things that my team members are either good at or like to do, because a good leader highlights and utilizes their team members' strengths and interests.

We all like to be comfortable. Sure, there are a few people who live in the world of discomfort, but most people want to live in the world of comfort. The question, though, is this: if I'm a servant leader—someone who sees their primary job as doing whatever it takes to empower their team members— whose comfort is more important? Mine or my team members'? I would argue that my team members' comfort is way more important than my comfort. Because, if I can allow them to work in their comfort zone, then they will be better team members. They will love showing up at work everyday; even better, they will recruit their friends. They will do a better job of customer service, and they will not change jobs to earn a quarter or fifty cents more an hour. That will make me, as a leader, less stressed out and happier, and increase my comfort level in the end.

> The highest form of leadership (Level 5 leadership), means the organization still thrives without you.
>
> —Jacquelyn Kung,
> CEO, Senior Care Group

I have thought a lot about why leaders are so reluctant to give autonomy. At the heart of it is a lack of trust. They don't trust the team members' skills and, even more importantly, they don't trust their judgement. But, if you peel back the layers of the onion it goes deeper. Those types of leaders probably never saw a successful model of autonomy in their journey. It may even be that those leaders are fearful that they are not capable of hiring team members who are worthy of autonomy. And, they assume, more emotionally than logically, that they can do everything better than their team members can.

Excellent leaders understand that they're smart about some things, but not so smart or capable in other areas. There's this idea that resonates with me: the very best leaders work hard to hire people who are smarter than themselves. They then turn those people loose to be amazing in their jobs. The end result is often even better than what the leader would have been able to accomplish. The challenge in all of this is that the end result will likely look different than what the leader envisioned or would have created. This can be pretty uncomfortable.

Fairly early in the life cycle of Senior Living Foresight, I tried my hand at podcasting. It was okay, but my efforts were primitive, so the success was very limited, and eventually I lost interest. It was an experiment that died a merciful death. Then, a year or so ago, it became clear that a podcast was something I needed to take another shot at, although my new vision was not much different or better than my previous one.

I got to talking to Pam about it. Her passion for it was about a hundred times greater than mine, so I handed it off to her. At first, I tried to tell her how to do it but she was not having it. Finally, I stopped my meddling and she laid out her plan. I was nervous and skeptical, but I promised to let her run it. I stepped back and said, "You're the boss, just tell me when you need me." She did, and the result is amazing. It's very different and so much better than what I had envisioned.

This all requires serious self-reflection: how do you know what you're smart about or good at? Unless you start there, you have no idea what to delegate, and you can't give people the autonomy they need for them, and you, to be successful. Having a clear vision of where they want to go and what they want to accomplish is critical to delegating. At the same time, being willing to change direction, if the evidence suggests that you need to do that, is critical. This might happen because you got it wrong or because somebody has shown you a better way.

A few months ago I was in Canada delivering a keynote address. Before the event, I was in a small group; someone asked me a question and I started responding to them. Another person looked at me with some amazement and asked, "How do you know all that stuff?"

I wish I could say it is because I am brilliant, but it's not that. The reason I know all this stuff is because I spent a lot of time thinking about what it means to be a great leader. I spent a lot of time wondering how I can be better about teaching leadership concepts. I ask myself, "How do I give people the ability to take what they know and turn it into something that results in wonderful organizations?" Maybe most importantly, I always have the sense that I don't know as much as I should or would like to know. I'm also willing to accept the fact that there will always be things I'm wrong about.

There is this notion that we make people feel better and help them be more competent by giving them more education. The big idea is that, by teaching them more, we are allowing them to be more independent. It seems logical but it turns out that doesn't work very well. For example, the United States has an impending doctor shortage; we know it is coming. The question is this: how do we fix the problem? The typical path a doctor follows is four years of college with a super heavy dose of biology, chemistry, and other foundational courses. Then comes four years of medical school, with the first year being mostly classroom work and each subsequent year becoming increasingly clinical. This is followed by a number of years of residency that leads to a specialization.

Imagine, instead, an alternate reality for training physicians. One where they would still go to school for the foundational classwork but then each future physician would spend the next four years shadowing another doctor in whatever specialization that interested them. These candidates would watch and learn and then be allowed, over time, to start hands-on training with the mentor physician. My guess is that we would substantially reduce the cost of training doctors and we would end up with better physicians who have more real-world experience.

When I think about the senior living sector, I have this picture of bringing in someone who wants to be an executive director in a situation similar to the alternate reality described above. The first day would take place over coffee and lunch and the conversation would only focus on culture and values, with the goal of making sure there is philosophical alignment between the candidate and organization. From that point on, the candidate would shadow the executive director for a year before they are turned loose. During that year, they would watch what's being done and then try some things. As they try those new things, they would learn what works for them, and gain confidence to do things a little differently. The executive director doing the mentoring would also be watching and learning from the candidate. Ultimately, both would grow.

The problem with classroom training in just about any industry is that it does nothing to teach people the tricks of the trade... all the little things that great leaders and professionals do that are not taught in the classroom—the unconventional things that actually work better than what we learn from books.

I taught flying when I was in college. You have to be a pretty good pilot and an okay teacher to get a flight instructor's license. That would have described my skill set on the day I took on my first student: pretty good pilot and decent teacher. What was so great about being an instructor, though, was that I also became a much better pilot. I would sit in the right seat of an airplane and ask student pilots to do things and it wouldn't work the way I wanted or expected it to. It was a bit like looking in a mirror. It allowed me to see my mistakes and why I was making them, which then gave me the ability to adjust my teaching methods.

When we turn people loose and give them autonomy, we end up with better systems and better results. Rather than doing things the same way over and over again, we're constantly striving to improve. To teach something is, perhaps, the best way to get really good at something.

I gave a two-hour keynote speech that included two interactive exercises. As I looked at the feedback I received after giving the presentation, a frequent comment was that the best part of my whole speech were those two exercises. As a group, people experienced the most growth during those twenty minutes than they did in the rest of the two-hour keynote because they were actually participating in their own learning, rather than just listening to my brilliant words.

Without giving your team autonomy, they can't experience that type of growth. If all you ever do as a leader is tell me what to do without giving me some independence, I'm going to get crazy frustrated. That will cause me to do one of two things: either I will leave your organization and tell everybody how much your organization sucks. Or, even worse, I will stay and sabotage your organization. I am convinced that this is the number one reason why flying on most of the major airlines has become a miserable experience.

If you want to see this in action fly on American Airlines. I hate flying American because their employees mostly hate their jobs, which means that they hate management, and they hate management for good reason. I want to make it clear that I am primarily talking here about C-Suite, policy-deciding management and not particularly mid-level managers who mostly have very little control. It is clear to me that management sees both the employees and the customers as adversaries; it is a very "us versus them" mentality. Their goal is to provide the least amount of money and authority possible to their team and simultaneously extract the most work they can get out of them. It is the same with passengers, who they see not as valued partners but as "in the flesh" ATMs, where they want to give them as little as the law will allow while sucking as much money as possible from them. They might even argue that this is as American (the country, not the airline) as apple pie, that it is the free-market way of doing things. It *is* a free-market way of doing things. Here is the problem: when you treat team members this way, they have only one way of getting their revenge against "the man," and that is to treat the customers poorly.

When you see people (customers or team members) only as an economic cost or a piggy bank, you are going to give them the least you can. On the flip side, if you view them as an investment, you'll treat them better than that. A few months ago my partner in some leadership development work I do, Denise Boudrou-Scott, and I took a small group of leaders to In-N-Out Burger University to learn why, in the fast food universe of 100 percent annual turnover rates, theirs is only in the 20 percent range. A big part of it is that they believe, with all their heart and soul, that they are the best burger company in the world. They believe they have the best burgers, the best fries, the best shakes, the best service, the freshest food, and the coolest way of doing things. They talk about and celebrate and remind each other often that they are better than everybody else. This, along with other things they do, does actually make them better than everybody else.

I teach a group of fifth- and sixth-grade kids at church. Every week, I remind them that they are the best, most caring, spiritual Junior class in the whole wide world. Are they actually that much better than anybody else? No, they're not... at least when I started doing this, they were not. Except for this: they are my kids and to me, they're better than any other group of fifth and sixth graders. This is just one of the things I do to get them to start thinking about themselves differently. After a while, they may very well be the best group of fifth- and sixth-grade church kids in the whole world. As an industry, as an organization, as a team, that's the key. If you tell your team they are the best in the world, that they provide the best service, or that they have the most innovative ideas, they are going to internalize that. Pretty soon, it will be true.

Every day each employee makes a decision: whether or not to come to work. That decision is, in part, a reflection of how they feel about their organization, Sure, many people go to work every day even though they hate their jobs and their organizations. Often they do so because they don't have the initiative to look for a new job, or there aren't any jobs out there, or it's scary to find a new job and they don't think the new job will be any better than the old job. When I think about this it drives me crazy. Why would anyone want to run an organization with employees who think like that?

In reality, most companies operate this way. They get away with seeing their employees as simply a cost center, rather than an investment. I recently had a team member who was trying to decide whether he wanted to continue working as part of my team or go do something else. He was struggling to fit in with my organization and our culture. If I just saw him as a cost, I would have cut my losses and turned him loose. Instead, my heart's desire was to help him and allow him to figure out what was best for himself. If that meant staying and growing with my organization, that was cool. If he wanted to go someplace else, then I wanted to help him figure out what that was and help him get there. I was investing in him, which was important to him, to me, and to the organization. As long as he is part of the organization, he is going to work hard at what we're doing because he knows I've got his back and I see him as a valuable part of the team.

We all want to be valued. While it's true that everybody is replaceable (except maybe the founder in smaller organizations), in top-performing companies team members are seen as a hugely valuable, even precious, asset. It puzzles me when organizations get rid of team members who need extra help or coaching. It means you have completely wasted whatever you have invested in them to that point in the relationship. If you as the leader are willing to work with the struggling team member, continue to invest in them. Give them appropriate autonomy and you will end up with a better team member. If they see that you believe in them, they will believe in themselves and in you.

And yet, there are times when a struggling team member needs to exit from an organization. My criteria for making that decision is pretty simple:

1. Do they see the problem? Are they willing to listen, learn, and grow? Are they willing to be mentored?
2. Do they have both the capacity and the willingness to grow and learn?
3. Over time, do you see evidence that significant progress is being made?

If you can't answer yes to those questions the situation will always get worse, not better. Once you see the problem can't be fixed in a timely fashion—or at all—you should part ways sooner rather than later. It is a tough balance, but I mostly see organizations hanging on too long more often than jumping the gun.

Have you ever been in a situation where you were communicating something to someone and, when you were done, they looked at you and said, "Sorry, could you repeat that?" Or, worse, they placated you by saying, "Yep. Uh huh. Got it," and you knew they weren't paying attention? It is frustrating, because it's clear that the person you were talking to was not really listening to you. Maybe they were distracted, or they didn't care about what you were trying to communicate. Perhaps the issue lies in your ability to communicate but, more often than not, the real issue is their inability to actively listen.

This is a very bad habit that many leaders have when team members try to communicate with them. It sends the message of "You don't really matter enough for me to give you my undivided attention" to the people they lead. A close cousin to this problem is that many leaders hear the words, acknowledge what was said, but don't actually do anything with what they are being told. If they hear what I have to say but they don't *do* anything with it, as in they don't implement my suggestions or at least consider them, then I'm going to feel like I don't matter and that they don't care. It's the same for your employees. Part of giving them that autonomy and demonstrating your trust is being willing to try out their ideas and actively listen when they come to you with questions or suggestions.

Here is an example of what this looks like in real life: I was asked to do some coaching for an executive director of a prominent and successful senior living community. Though the community he was leading was full, it had terrible employee turnover rates and poor morale. While many of the team members would describe him as a nice person, they didn't like him or feel close to him. Most importantly, they did not trust him as a leader. There were a bunch of reasons for distrust, but the single biggest reason was that team members felt like he would not listen to them. When I sat with him and talked about this, he insisted that the employees were all wrong and that he was a good listener who talked to his team members every day. He was intent on proving it and told me that, since it was time for him to make rounds, I should follow him and watch.

Our first stop was the employee break room where two front-line team members were hanging out, one from dining services and the other a care aide. The executive director walked in and asked, "Hey, how's it going?" When they said, "Good," he reacted by saying, "Okay, see you later," and started out the door. That was it.

I saw a teachable moment for him (and maybe myself) so I jumped in and asked the team members a question: "What is one thing that would make your job better?" In an instant, each one had a great suggestion. One could be implemented immediately and the other represented a fair concern that would have been reasonably easy to address. The economic cost for both suggestions was just pocket change in terms of the community budget.

As the leader and I walked out of the room he turned to me and said, "See? I listen!" In reality, he didn't. He heard the words, but dismissed them in his head immediately. The message he sent to those team members was that he didn't care about them or their suggestions. He cared about his own ego, his own agenda, and making himself look good. His actions were worse than neutral; he made the team members—at some level—trust him a little less.

Developing active listening skills should be critical for executive leadership, because that executive director was an extension of the C-suite. Even though, in this case, it was not true, he'd sent the message to those team members that top-level management didn't care about them. Peeling the onion back one more layer, disrespecting those suggestions was another way of saying, "I actually don't care about the quality of the work being done here."

Earlier in this chapter I talked about working with people if they are willing to see changes that need to be made and are willing to work on those areas. I am sorry to say, this leader was completely unwilling to do either. He is no longer a part of that organization, and I believe they waited much too long to turn him loose.

Inferiority Complex

In the senior living industry, and I suspect this is true in some other industry sectors, we have a major inferiority complex. We tell ourselves that we're not smart enough, we're not good enough leaders, our technology isn't good enough, and the only way we're ever going to get better is if we spend all our time looking at what people outside our industry are doing.

We try to learn from those other industries because we think they're a lot smarter and better at everything than we are. I know this sector forward and backward. If I wanted to be negative, I could write a book on what is wrong with senior living. But, in truth, it is an amazing part of the elder care and health care economies that provide jobs and improve the lives of millions of people every day.

Don't get me wrong, it's important to look at what other companies are doing inside and outside your core sector and learn from them. It's important to look at other cultures to learn from them and figure out how you can adopt their best practices. We know our sector better than anybody else. We understand the challenges, we understand the opportunities, and if we actually believed in ourselves, we'd be better off and more successful.

This same concept applies to you and your team. Instead of looking outside your organization or your business for solutions to problems... talk to your team. They know your culture, they know your industry, and they know more about your organization than anyone else could. They likely know more about your organization than you do! I guarantee they know things you don't know—but should know—that would make you a better leader of a better organization.

Try this: sit with your team and ask, "What would it take to make our organization or our senior living community or even our department an eleven-star organization, community, or department? What would we have to do to make people feel blown away when they have an experience with us? What would we have to do to get our community full with a waiting list, and to have people standing in line to come work with us?"

Then, sit back and listen. You probably can't do this with your whole team, but it would be smart to break your dining team, for example, into two or three groups, and sit down and talk about what an eleven-star experience would be for dining. Then, do the same thing with your care team, the front office, and your sales and marketing team.

In too many organizations, there is this notion that the best ideas come from the leadership team and that, the further up the leadership hierarchy you go, the better ideas you'll find. They believe that all ideas should flow down from the top. Then they expect the team members who are doing the heavy lifting to be excited about those ideas. That would be great... if it worked. In practice, it's a terrible way to move the organization forward no matter how good the ideas or initiatives are, no matter how noble the intent. If there is no ownership there will be no buy-in because the team members won't feel any connection to the ideas.

You may be thinking, "Wait a minute, it's the job of the leaders and the leadership team to come up with ideas." There's no doubt that this is true and, ultimately, many of the best and biggest ideas *will* flow from the top. But improving the organization also requires getting buy-in from the team. To do this, when you have an idea, float it out to the team with an explanation of why you think the idea should be implemented, and explain what you are trying to accomplish. Describe how it will benefit the team, benefit the customers, and benefit the organization. Then ask, "What do you think?" If you *actively listen* to what they have to say, one of three things will happen:

1. They will love the idea and be fully on board (almost never the case).
2. They will hate the idea and tell you why it is dumb (also almost never the case but if it happens, you need to pay attention).
3. They will tell you how to make your great idea even better (the most likely outcome).

A tiny detour: If #2 happens it will tell you one of two things: the first, and most likely, is that they are right and it is a bad idea. But, once in awhile, it will be a good idea and they will still hate it. This should be a huge red flag that you have massive culture problems. It likely means you have some people on your team who are toxic and need to move on to a different organization.

Conversely, when you start to implement some of your team's suggestions and they help you get to that eleven-star experience, they can say, "I did that." They can say, "I helped make this happen," "I'm a part of something bigger," and "What I do really matters, really makes a difference."

Technology Inferiority

The inferiority complex in the senior living industry is rampant, but nowhere is it more alive than where technology fits in the senior living space. In truth, this is an area where we have been lacking, but not as much, or as badly, as we believe.

Over the past ten to fifteen years, almost every industry has experienced massive technological improvements. The reality of senior living is that it's a people business, meaning it is a human business, a high-touch business with one-on-one caregiving and small-group activities. Because of this, we don't work with a lot of technology. Perhaps rather than feeling like we are inferior, we should embrace a bit of an anti-technology bias knowing that the single biggest risk of technology is that it reduces human interaction.

Don't get me wrong, there are places where technology provides huge value. For a few years, I worked as a salesperson for Vigil Health Solutions, a great British Columbia, Canada technology company that sold high-end emergency call systems. I was making sales calls in the Pacific Northwest and I called on a community where the call system was essentially a string tied to a tennis ball. That string ran up to a series of eye hooks in the ceiling, then back to a call cord on the wall. The tennis balls were strung from the bed, the bathroom, or an easy chair.

It was about as technologically backward as you could get and looked super funky, but it worked. Sometimes, that's all you need. You don't need to sink a ton of money into technology just because you feel inferior about your industry or your organization. It is unlikely that someone will choose to do business with you solely or primarily because you have the latest and greatest technology. Sometimes all you really need is a tennis ball on a string.

Too often we unnecessarily worry that, if we're not the next Google or Facebook or Disney, customers won't want to use our services and no one will want to work for us because we are backward or outdated.

Listen to your employees when they suggest areas in your organization that could use an update or a change, but don't make changes for the sole sake of keeping up with other industries.

Chapter 7

Be Best Buddies with Your Sales and Marketing Team

Let's start with your salespeople.

Being a front-line salesperson is often the hardest job emotionally, in any senior living community. Many salespeople feel like no matter how good they are it is never good enough. They also feel like they are one lost sale from losing their job. If you are not frequently interacting with them, they get paranoid. And no one does a good job when they are paranoid.

When they are not performing, they feel that at least in part it is your fault. They tend to believe that if you, as a leader, created a better environment, if you did a better job operationally, or if your product offerings or your pricing were better, then they would have an easier time being successful. It is critical that executive directors make their salespeople their best work friends.

There is a sense that as a salesperson, I am only as good as my last sale. There is some truth in this. Imagine you are an executive director and you have been handed a brand-new, but empty, senior living community with one hundred apartments. You also have on your team an amazing salesperson and a hot market. In just four months that salesperson takes your community from zero occupancy to 100 hundred percent.

You are so ecstatic about that salesperson that they can have most anything they want. They are the hero of your community and your whole organization. Your community is making buckets of money and you are earning top bonuses. Then suddenly something happens and you lose your mojo. Six months go by and you haven't moved anybody in and your bottom line is suffering and your bonuses have disappeared. It all becomes that salesperson's fault. You don't care—no one cares—that six months ago you were full in four months. That success isn't worth squat anymore. You're scared and worried, and you put pressure on your salesperson who is even more scared and stressed than you are. This, in turn, tanks their selling skills even further, making things even harder.

There are two truths I've discovered in my leadership and service to others. First, there are days we pick the grapes together, and days we drink the wine. You never know when you may be humbled by the hard work in the vineyard and who will be with you. Never take for granted how much effort is needed to cultivate a vintage wine. Secondly, we pay either way. We can make money or we can lose money. In the business of caring for people, investing in our associates pays off in fulfilling every metric of senior living success.

—Fara Gold McLaughlin,
Founder and CEO of GoldMark Seniors

Feeling Safe

Building a relationship with your salespeople is all about making your team members feel safe. A feeling of safety means that instead of wasting their energy on worrying, all their energy and effort will go into doing their job well. Sometimes salespeople really do see things that you and your operations team members are missing. They have the ability to help your organization become better and to solve problems. But if you don't actively listen to them and all you do is tell them to "Go sell more," I can guarantee you are missing opportunities that will make it easier for them to close business, improve your bottom line, and make you look good to your superiors.

Almost every human being is a quivering mass of insecurity. Particularly when it comes to salespeople. They tend to be overachievers who mask their particular version of insecurity by being good at selling. The number of sales they make and the amount of revenue they generate is the scorecard that shows the world, and themselves, how good they are. Selling anything is an emotional exercise and this is particularly true with senior living. I'm not talking just about the prospects, but about the salespeople themselves—they have to be highly emotional to relate to the prospects and help them make difficult choices. This means your sales and marketing people need buckets of emotional support. Their self-confidence needs to be nurtured and cared for. This is important because, if they believe they are a great salesperson, then they are more likely to be successful. Success helps reinforce that belief, which leads to more success.

There are two ways to feel like a great salesperson. The first is to make a lot of sales, but even then one might not feel like a great salesperson, feeling instead like they just got lucky. The second is for leaders to continually remind their salespeople that they are great at what they do, and to talk with great specificity about *how* they are great at it. Don't get me wrong, this is maybe the most important thing, but it will not do any good if you don't also give them other tools they need to do the best job possible.

Storytelling

Storytelling is critical to sales in senior living. If you were to visit a community as a prospect, after being offered cookies and coffee, you would be handed a detailed booklet full of every feature and amenity the marketing folks thought of. A senior living community needs to do this, because the prospect has come to expect it and they may feel cheated if they aren't handed something that makes them feel good.

But, here is the problem: if you were to go to one hundred communities you would find the features would be almost the same at every single one. Even worse, most of those amenities would not be what you really cared about.

For most prospects today, particularly when they are looking for assisted living or memory care, safety, security, and high-quality care are the big hot buttons. No matter which of those one hundred communities you walk into, you won't find a single salesperson who says, "Our community is just average" or, "I don't think you would really like it here." Every single one of them will tell you their community is the greatest place for seniors to live out their last chapters. The question then is, how do good sales and marketing people make your community stand out? They use social proof. In other words, they tell stories. Not about who the leaders are, or the location, or the amenities, but about the residents, the quality of care they receive, and the marvelous, transformative lives they live.

It goes something like this: "Lori moved into our community a month ago, and she did not want to move in. Her family was so concerned for her because since she quit driving she lost all connection with her friends and seemed to be getting more depressed by the day. As unhappy as she was living at home she *did not want to move*. Her family more or less forced the move to happen. Sounds pretty terrible, right? But look at her today. That is her right over there, with the smile on her face, surrounded by her friends. She and her family would tell you that her moving here is one of the best decisions she made, even though she didn't really make it."

Or, in a nursing home it might look like this: "Mabel came into this building with a speech problem and no one could get her to talk. The family, doctors, and speech therapists tried everything they could think of and it was all a big bust. Then, she moved into our nursing center and, after a month of working with our speech therapist and getting better nutrition, she started talking again. I just about cried when I watched Mabel, who hadn't spoken to her family for six months, finally speak to them. Her great-granddaughter ran up and hugged her. Mabel looked at her with a huge grin and said, 'I love you'."

The problem is, your salespeople often are so busy selling that they don't get to see this stuff happen. But, other members of your staff do. Those salespeople need to hear about those stories because it gives them a purpose and keeps them going. Equally as important is that those stories become powerful tools that can be used as arrows in their quiver when they interact with prospects.

In senior living, we know that location is the primary reason families choose the communities their loved ones move into. At the same time, we know they are willing to drive right past closer options if they believe their loved one will be significantly happier or better cared for in a community that takes longer to get to. Using storytelling is the best way for you to differentiate your community. Since your sales team mostly can't be there to collect these stories, it falls on you as the leader to gather them, sometimes get them into usable form, and then pass them along.

I often ask leaders to tell me a story about a resident, family member, or team member who has been impacted by the community or the organization. A story that will make me laugh, cry, or cringe, or that represented a learning experience.

It distresses me almost beyond words that, most of the time, a leader will respond with something like this: "There are just so many stories…" followed by a long, long silence until: "I can't think of one right off the top of my head." Every time this happens, my heart breaks. In fact, nothing about senior living frustrates me more than this.

Every single leader should have two or three stories ready to tell. How can you, as a leader, support your marketing team emotionally and also give them the tools they need to succeed? The key is to meet with families and residents yourself. Build your own stories. Visit your facilities, meet with every prospective resident. For one, that prospect probably doesn't trust salespeople, but when they get to meet the executive director and see what kind of person they are, it helps increase sales. It also becomes a story you can share with your team.

Everybody is a storyteller, it seems to be something we are born with. We don't know why this is true, but we tend to enjoy telling disaster stories more than we tell happy stories. Like this:

I was reading a Facebook post where someone was lamenting being stuck in a middle seat when flying from New York to Phoenix. His post ran for two paragraphs about how terrible it was to be in the middle seat in the back of the plane.

He received a ton of responses, including one from me. Here is what's fascinating about his post: in the scope of problems in the world and problems in people's lives, being stuck in a middle seat in the back of an airplane for five hours is hardly worth being a story. Every single day tens of thousands of people are stuck in middle seats in the back of the plane. Right now as you are reading this, thousands of people are stuck in middle seats and not happy about it at all. The bigger story, the more amazing story is that that morning he got up, drove to the airport, climbed into a big silver tube, and five hours later walked out of that tube two thousand miles away in Phoenix! One story happy, the other grumpy.

In order for that happy story to be told, it has to be much more impactful. Otherwise we don't tell it. If I go to a restaurant and somebody brings me my hamburger and it's got all the condiments the first time and I've got all my silverware and my water stays full, that's not an exciting story. That doesn't happen very often, but that's never a story that I'm going to tell because that's what I expect.

We want people telling the good stories, not the bad stories, whether it's an employee or a resident or a family member. To achieve that, we have to create amazing experiences that are worth telling stories about. We also need to be the storytellers. As storytellers, we can take those little moments that other people wouldn't see as being worthy of sharing and we can craft them into great stories. As we start looking for those moments and telling those stories, other people start doing the same. It's about taking the micro moments and magnifying them and talking about how great they were.

Sometimes, supporting your sales and marketing staff comes in the form of emotional support, sometimes it's about making them feel safe and secure in their job, sometimes it's about connecting with them through stories, and sometimes it's about giving them the tools and knowledge they need to close the sale. Whatever form it comes in, giving them your support will be the best thing you can do for the success of your organization.

Chapter 8

Educate Yourself

My father is almost ninety years old. By his own admission, he was not the best dad in the world to me and my brother when we were growing up. But the one gift he gave me that surpasses all others is the gift of curiosity. Not everyone has that. I could be fascinated by the schematics of a washing machine because I want to find out how it works. (Although my wife says I wouldn't be interested in actually operating it.) I once saw a story about a weird kind of shark that had been found on the beach somewhere like Madagascar. I spent thirty minutes researching the shark because it caught my interest. Curiosity must be embraced; it can be nurtured and grown because it's about asking questions. You start by asking, "What are the facts about this thing?" Then you go to a deeper level—this is ultimately the most important part of it—and you ask, "What does this mean?"

As a blogger, I have a unique writing style that is very personal and that resonates with my readers. It makes people curious. People always want to know how I produce all of that content... how do I think of that stuff? I wish I could tell you that I have a crystal ball or a magic formula that makes it work, but the truth is that it comes from being a very curious person. I take in lots of information; I probably read ten to twenty leadership books a year and look at thousands of articles online. I have conversations with thousands of people a year about leadership and senior living. I take all that stuff in where it rattles around my brain along with the overarching perpetual question: "What does this mean?" "What does this mean to senior living?" Then, as a writer, publisher, and speaker, I take one more step and ask myself, "How can I process this information in a way that will help people be better leaders?"

As I talk to senior living providers, particularly those on the frontline, I find they are so busy running their particular enterprise that they don't feel like they have time to read things, think about things, and then process those things.

> Most of us have a lot of time that we waste every day.
> —Steve Moran

I am going to ruffle some feathers here, but in reality most of us have a lot of time that we waste every day. Most businesspeople check their email an astonishing 150 times a day... I am likely one of them. Then, there is the time they spend on Facebook, Instagram, and watching television. According to a March 1, 2018 article on Inc.com titled "New Study Shows You're Wasting 21.8 hours a Week", the average business executive wastes more than twenty-one hours each week. This is not a typical forty-hour work week, but rather a week in which the executive is working sixty-plus hours.

While we have more time than we realize, we only have a limited amount of energy that we can put into things. So the challenge really is this: how do you manage the energy you spend? What's curious is that, if leaders invested more time in nurturing their curiosity, reading books, watching TED talks, looking at articles about the industry and outside the industry, they would find they have more time and energy... and would be more successful.

I, of course, think every leader ought to be reading everything that Senior Living Foresight publishes, but they have to be looking at other industry publications as well as those outside the senior living sector. My favorites include *Fast Company, Inc., Forbes,* and the *Wall Street Journal.* Each provides a different perspective on leadership. As I explore these resources I find myself contemplating what I am reading, listening to, and watching means for senior living. I'm more often surprised than not.

Recently, we published an article in which I talked about whether or not the demise of Toys "R" Us might have some lessons for senior living. Specifically, I explored how we might be facing similar risk factors or dangers. Here is what I came up with:

It's conventional wisdom that Toys "R" Us died primarily because of Amazon, but also because the big-box retailers like Walmart and Target had their own toy sections. While these were factors, maybe it is not quite that simple or inevitable.

I postulated that perhaps what happened was that they got starved for cash and weren't able to innovate and change with the marketplace... that they were unable to continue making stores more appealing to kids and parents. After all, there is no question that kids would rather visit a real toy store and put their hands on the toys, than look at a catalog or shop online. Toy stores should be appealing and exciting to kids, and at the same time delight parents and grandparents. Toys "R" Us was a complete failure at doing this. Maybe they lacked inspiration and drive, but it is also possible they simply lacked the cash to execute.

I then asked if my industry, senior living, faces the same challenges.

Curiosity is something that's honed over time. The more curious you are, the more curious you become. I've noticed some similar traits that successful, curious people share.

- They surround themselves with other curious people.
- They have the courage to experiment.
- They're willing to be wrong and they're willing to change their mind.
- They are willing to listen to their critics.
- They are willing to go out of their way to get information that may be of opposing views.
- They step back and ask themselves, "What does this mean?"

It is important to nurture curiosity by surrounding yourself with other people who are willing to ask tough questions. Curious leaders have the courage to be wrong and the courage to change their minds as they get new information, new ideas, and hear about new ways of doing things. I love the idea that strong curious leaders have "strong opinions that are loosely held," something most often attributed to Paul Saffro, director of Palo Alto's Institute for the Future, but also attributed to A.J.P. Taylor. As a blog publisher, this is a high-value principal for me. I have written more than one blog where I had to revisit what I wrote and say, "I was wrong." It's usually not a matter of me being factually wrong—which while inevitable, is never good, but rather a situation where I had an idea and held an opinion but, as more information came in, I had to change my position.

Early in the life of my blog *Senior Living Foresight* I wrote a post in which I suggested ageism was just another stupid, overly politically correct idea for people to get mad about. My conclusion was that it was not worth talking about or spending any time thinking about. But, weirdly, writing about it as something to be dismissed actually got me thinking more about it and reading more about it and I came to realize that ageism *is* a big deal. It is important and it is a real problem. When I wrote the article, I truly believed that it was a stupid thing, but I wasn't so dogmatically tied into this belief that no matter what the evidence, I wouldn't change my mind. It was a strong opinion, weakly held.

It also meant that, since I had a new way of thinking about it, I had to write a new blog post talking about my new thinking and how I got there.

Curious leaders must be willing to listen to their critics. More than that, they have to embrace their critics. They don't always have to agree with them, but they have to say, "Okay, this person is a critic and, even if they are a jerk, what can I learn from what they're saying? Maybe there are some lessons here." This means being willing to go out of their way to engage with people and ideas that they are fundamentally, and maybe even morally, opposed to. It does not mean you need to agree—often you won't—but even then you might learn something important.

The vocal opposition provides a much better understanding of what the "right" answer is. You will often find that people who are philosophically opposed actually have some common ground with you and, even reasonable ideas. If you're politically liberal, you should spend some time listening to Rush Limbaugh and Sean Hannity. If you're politically conservative, you should spend some time reading Barack and Michelle Obama's books. This means being open and really listening to their ideas, not just looking for all the things you disagree with. It will give you a broader perspective. It will give you the ability to think about things differently. Curious people continually step back and ask:

- What does that mean?
- How does what I am reading, listening to, watching, thinking about impact my life?
- Do I need to be adjusting my mission in life… my purpose in life?
- How can I use what I am thinking about to help other people?

What Does It Mean?

This is such an important question to ask. Knowledge, without asking what it means, is a pastime. It is like training for a race but never racing. Asking yourself "What does this mean?" gives you the ability to take a whole bunch of separate pieces of information and integrate them into a fantastic tapestry. Until you ask *What does this mean?*, you can't use your accumulated information to change the world, which we are ultimately all called to do.

If you don't use it or take action, then what was the point? Why take in that information, all those incredible ideas, if you're not going to use them?

It would be like reading leadership book after leadership book, learning about what motivates people and demotivates people, and then never doing anything about it. And yet, I am fearful that this is what happens mostly. People have access to all this amazing information but they don't use it. That's why we have so few exemplary organizations out there. Or, maybe more fairly and accurately, some people will take one tiny idea and try it, usually the easy stuff. Then, when they get tiny results or no results, they give up.

What does it mean to use this accumulated knowledge to make your organization better? Different people are going to have different ideas about that. Most commonly the answer is: the organization will be more profitable. For other people, it might be the ability to serve the most people in the best way possible. In the senior living industry, it is improving the lives of our residents and our team members.

Curiosity is a lifestyle. At ninety-plus my father continues to be a living example of this as one of the most curious people I know. Nobody would ever blame him if, at ninety years old, he said, "You know, I'm never going to read another book or look at another article. I'm just going to watch TV. I'm done growing, I've done enough of that." No one would judge him if he decided to be done learning new things. You could even argue that at his age, it is a waste of his time and effort, a waste of the relatively small amount of time he has left on this planet, learning things he will likely never use anyway. But for him it's a lifestyle. Curiosity is an inextricable part of who he is.

If you are not a curious person you are likely not reading this book. If you are a curious person it may be that you need to be nurturing that curiosity; growing it. There is good evidence suggesting that people who are curious and continue to learn are exercising their brain, and that by doing this, you will at least significantly slow the progression of Alzheimer's.

Recently, I made a video that came out of something I was reading because I was so curious about it. It got me to thinking that pretty much every video I do, every article I write, every speech I give, even this book, are all based on things I read or learn. In a very real sense, nothing I ever create is original because it always comes from a conversation I've had or a book I've read.

In that particular video, I proposed that leaders ought to spend time with each of their direct reports and ask them one question: What's something that we should be doing that would make our organization more profitable?

This question not only has the potential to give you some great new ideas but it also sends some important messages to your team members including: "I care about what you think. I'm going to actually listen to your ideas. I am going to process and follow up with you about what you are thinking."

Don't get me wrong, not all their ideas will be that great and even some great ideas won't be practical, but this makes no difference. Some ideas will be good, and a few will even be amazing. Just asking the question will make them more curious and will get their creative juices flowing. Some of the ideas may seem scary or stupid. Are there risks? Before I tried it with my team at Senior Living Foresight I worried they would tell me I should stop doing some things I'm doing and that I would not like their answers very much. And yet, they had the real potential to change what we were doing and ultimately change the world.

It is important to keep educating yourself, asking questions, and really listening to people when they talk. Being open to new ideas is the cornerstone of growth.

Educating yourself doesn't always come in the form of books and conferences. Sometimes you learn the most by talking with people. When I first started Senior Living Foresight, I was this guy who just put content out there and hoped people would read it. As it started to grow and the blog got traffic, I realized how much I didn't know. Stuff about publishing and business.

I didn't have anyone to bounce ideas around with. I wrote an article and this guy Dennis McIntee reached out and we developed a relationship. Dennis was a lot farther down the road in his journey so, suddenly, I had this guy I could piggyback off of. Then I ran into this woman, Denise Scott, at a conference where she slugged me in the arm because she thought I was somebody else. She was horribly embarrassed when she realized her mistake, and then we ended up talking more and she became another friend, another person to start bouncing ideas off of.

At that point in time, my organization was essentially just me. I needed people to talk to, people I could feel comfortable enough with to say, "I don't know what to do here," or "I have this idea, what do you think?" Or, they could come to me and I could do the same thing for them.

Today we have an interdependent relationship where no single person has all the answers. When I meet people who believe they are smart and that they do hold all the answers, I get nervous. The biggest fear that I have in leading an organization, and honestly the biggest thing any leader should fear, is that leaders don't know the stuff they don't know. When I *know* that I don't know something, that's okay. When I *don't know* what I don't know, it's a very scary thing. Those are traps that can get you in deep trouble.

I didn't know what I didn't know. In my case, I didn't know how much money I should charge. I didn't know what stories to talk about. I didn't know how to grow my business, how to build an audience. In my business, I have two audiences to think about. The first audience, which is obvious, is the group of people who own and operate senior living communities. They will modify how they serve families and team members better and more efficiently. The second audience is the people who want to sell products and services to the senior living industry. How do I tell the story to them in a way that makes sense? Having people that I could discuss this with made it much easier.

Chapter 9

Know the Person You Report to

In any senior living community, a high-performing team starts with the executive director having a great relationship with the person to whom they directly report. In a small company that might be the CEO or COO; in a bigger company, that could be a regional executive director. If it's a good working relationship, the executive director knows that their supervisor has their back and is a great resource, and that corporate-level leader can trust that the executive director will make them look good.

All working relationships land somewhere on a continuum. On one end, there is no real personal relationship; it is just a paycheck and the time clock. On the other end, there is an overly friendly relationship where the boundaries between work and friendship are blurred.

There are dangers to having a tight friendship, just as there are dangers to a total lack of friendship. Ultimately, though, we know that when people have friends at work everything runs more smoothly. Team members are less likely to complain and more likely to recommend the workplace to their friends. As a leader in an organization, if you're working with people that you like and have fun with, enjoy, and trust, things go better and are more fun than if you were simply managing people or telling them what to do. Unfortunately, some leaders get a huge ego boost by not having friends and being able to boss team members around. They think it's pretty cool to be able to say, "I can treat these people like marionettes and make them jump." I hope there are not many like this. In the long run it causes more frustration than happiness. Worse, it often makes achieving company goals hard or impossible.

Most relationships in business tend to be more transactional than relational. It is likely getting worse every day, thanks to the internet. There are lots of good reasons for transactional relationships. We are all busy and, if time is the number one metric, nothing beats a transactional relationship.

Here is the problem: when they're transactional, they're adversarial. I am giving something to get something. I want to give as little as I have to while still getting the most I can. While I don't necessarily want to cheat the person I am transacting with, I also don't want to give up more than I must. The big assumption in a transactional relationship is that it's a zero-sum game.

It turns out that transactional relationships at work are pacts of mutual destruction and are amazingly inefficient. What works much better is being friends, or at least friendly, which turns into a tight alignment: having the same goals and wanting the same things. There is also never a single goal. The first goal, but not the only goal, and maybe not even the most important goal, is to make the business successful. But if I make the business successful on your back, that's not very nice or very fair and it likely will not last.

If I could pick one trait to magically instill in my fellow team members it would be trust. It's the key to everything that is possible.

—John Cochrane,
President and CEO of HumanGood

Ideally, I want to make the business successful *and* you successful, because in making you successful, I'm actually going to improve my business even more than if I take advantage of you. When you work for someone who knows you, who trusts you, and who will support you, you are delighted to go to work every day. Your job is fulfilling and rewarding because your "boss" reminds you of that; you're a friend and not just a transaction to them.

There are two ways to look at work. It is either a place where you earn a paycheck, or a place where you get personal fulfillment. I'm very fortunate in that I have a job where I work for myself, that gives me tremendous emotional fulfillment, and that I love doing. I'm not sure what it would be like if I hated doing what I do. Critically important is that I wouldn't be very good at what I do.

Each day when I get ready for work, I can hardly wait for the day or the week to start. Don't get me wrong, not everything is great fun. I still have to pay bills and chase late payments. I have to deal with problems and complaints. But then I look at what I get to do, the stuff that delights, that makes me want to pinch myself... that I get paid to do. Reading books, having conversations with leaders, and writing articles, books, and speeches. I'm not so crazy about the "paying the bills" part, not because I don't have the money to do it, it's just tedious stuff that needs to get done. I like entering checks and depositing those, but even that's not particularly fulfilling.

What I love is that I basically get paid to have conversations with thousands of people a year, and then I write about those conversations. That's how I make my living. But in the bigger picture, I am helping senior living organizations become better at what they do. In very real terms I am making the lives of seniors and team members better. *That's* hugely fulfilling. It's these things that keep me excited about going to work every day.

When work is transactional everyone feels used, used up, and taken advantage of. A personal example of this is from an experience I had on a cruise ship. I used my smartphone before going to bed one night. I couldn't find it the next morning, but I was on vacation so it was no big deal that I didn't have it. I figured the phone was buried in the sheets and that when the cabin was cleaned it would turn up and I would find it sitting on a shelf when we got back from a tour we were taking that day.

Logical thinking, except when we returned, it wasn't there. I did a more thorough search and it was nowhere to be found. My next thought was that we had room service for breakfast and that maybe I had left the phone on the tray. My wife called guest services and said, "Hey, we lost a cell phone and we're wondering if it might have ended up back in the kitchen." I had no thought at all that anyone but me had caused the problem. We were not mad, upset (though I was frustrated at myself), or accusatory.

About ten minutes later there was frantic banging on our door. It was our cabin steward; he was in a complete panic because we had called and said we lost the cell phone. His supervisors called him about it. Our cabin steward said, "You shouldn't have done that. You should have come to me first because now I'm in trouble."

This initially struck me as bizarre. I never thought for a moment that it was his fault. I was a bit worried that I had eaten breakfast on the balcony and maybe accidentally kicked the phone over the side of the ship and it was gone forever. The steward was worried to tears—terrified, even after we tried to explain that we knew it wasn't his fault. It was clear he was sure he was going to be accused and fired.

As I thought about it, I felt terrible for this poor guy! Here he was, worried that he would lose his job over something that was not his fault. I am sure it would have been an economic disaster for him and his family. Cruise ships see their lower-level workers as disposable commodities and don't really care about them, their lives, or their families. The steward was from Jamaica, and there are ten thousand people in Jamaica who are out of work, who would do a great job, and would be delighted if that position were to open up.

From the cruise line's perspective, it was likely only a minor annoyance to get rid of him and find another person to do that job, and it was clear he knew this to be true. In turn, it made him react in a horrible way. His reaction, in a very real way, was not his fault but rather that of the cruise line because they treated him as "less than." There was no sense of "Hey, we know you and we trust you that you didn't do this."

It was the exact opposite: "If the cell phone is missing, it must be your fault." As it turned out, I had put the phone on a shelf that was close to the floor and hard to see, where I finally found it. He may have still gotten fired even though we went out of our way to tell his supervisors it was all my fault and that we found it.

From an economic perspective this may have worked okay for the ship, because while I was not terribly fond of our cabin steward, how good or bad he was made little difference with respect to my overall cruise experience. And yet even in this situation, I wondered how much better it would have been if he did not live his life in fear.

In senior living though, these are long-term relationships; having a team member that primarily operates in a transactional mode that is fear-based has terrible consequences.

Chapter 10

If You're in An Impossible Situation, You Need to Change Jobs

This is a tough chapter to write, and tough medicine to take, but here it is:

> If you're in an impossible situation, you need to change jobs.

We only have one life to live, a limited number of hours and days in our lives. We spend at least as many waking hours at work as we spend in any other way. Why would you continue to work in an environment that makes you miserable? Doing so kills the soul one second at a time. Don't think I don't get it. Sometimes you have to put up with misery for a short period of time to pay the bills, but too many of us keep putting up with it when we don't need to.

I wish I could tell you that I think that every single person can go out and find a job that makes them blissfully happy. I'm very fortunate, I have a job like that as a writer and a blogger and a publisher. It took me decades—most of my working life—to get here and I've had some pretty terrible jobs along the way.

I was in Silicon Valley and I'd been out of work for a few months and needed a job. While not in immediate danger of being on the streets, paying the bills each month was a close call. I saw a job posting for a company I knew something about and I was a fit for the position. I also knew the company leadership was brutal, maybe immoral, but honestly, I was desperate.

I applied for the job and was invited in for an interview. It went well and they made me a job offer on the spot. I accepted even though I didn't want to. I was 99 percent sure I would hate it and that if I was still there a year after accepting the job I would likely be fired, but at least it was income for some number of months.

It was a sales job and it was impossible to be successful. Every year, for at least ten years, they'd hire somebody and then fire them a year later because they weren't successful. This happened year after year. While I had a tiny, tiny fantasy that I could do better, I had no real reason to believe that I would.

I spent the year doing the best that I could, though if I am honest with myself I didn't work as hard as I might have otherwise, because I knew what was going to happen. The job paid my bills for a year and I actually made it thirteen months before being handed my walking papers. Sometimes we do work that we have to, even if it's terrible.

I never had any illusions about that sales job being a successful career for me, but I also knew that it was a step toward getting me someplace else and it wouldn't be terrible forever. I wasn't *stuck* there forever.

Companies create—intentionally and accidentally—all kinds of golden handcuffs that make it hard for team members to leave their jobs. Hunting for a job is scary, hard, and emotionally difficult. It seems easier to stay where you are because it means not having to put yourself out there. But you need to ask yourself this question: if you can leave your job that sucks life and energy out of you and take a position where you're happy, why not do it?

Or, it might even be this. Your current job is a good one and fulfilling but you wish you had more time to do the things you love, creatively or philanthropically. You might very well leave your good job for a job that's less fulfilling but has a more flexible schedule so you can do the things you love. You may find yourself working in an environment where the leadership isn't very good, or you don't respect the leadership. In that case, it's time to get out. You won't succeed in that position and you will lose respect for yourself. Sometimes, we don't recognize exactly why a job isn't working, we just know we are unhappy, stressed, or anxious. Ask yourself three questions:

1. Why did I start working here in the first place? In the case of my Silicon Valley job, I started working there because I needed an income. That's not a sustainable reason to stay in a job you hate. You'll burn out eventually, regardless of how important that income is.

2. Am I good at this job? This can be a hard question to answer. It may very well be that you don't have the right skill set, or you may not have the right personality for that position in that company. It also may be as

simple as facing the reality that if you are miserable in your position you can't possibly be great at it. It could be that you can find the same position with similar duties in an organization you respect, and be great at what you do. If you are not good at your job, it is time to cut your losses and move on. Staying is not fair to you and not fair to the organization you are working for. There have been a couple of times when I accepted a job and it turned out I wasn't very good at it. I wasn't a great Silicon Valley sales guy. I wasn't terrible, but I was not great. It wasn't a fit for me.

3. Do I like this job? If the answer is no, then you have a few more questions you need to ask yourself. Why don't I like this job? Is it the people I am working with or for? Is there something I need to change in myself?

As you answer these questions, pay attention to where you're placing blame for your problems. I'll give you an example. A friend of mine had been in a key position at a senior living organization for about a year. Objectively, it was a tough organization to work for. I would talk to her over the months about how it was going and it was all bad, bad, bad. She was very unhappy. Then, a few weeks ago, we were talking and she said, "You know, it's kind of a funny thing, but I realized that there's one person to whom I've been venting that added fuel to the fire of my frustration because they're also very negative. Maybe if I didn't spend so much time talking to them, I'd have discovered sooner that it wasn't the organization that was the issue, it was me and my attitude."

> We all need to be willing to self-evaluate. Maybe I'm the problem, not the organization.
>
> —Steve Moran

It's a tough thing to do, but we all have to stop and think, maybe the problem isn't the organization, maybe it's me. That doesn't mean you don't need to change jobs. Sometimes you get into a toxic environment where things have gone so far down the rabbit hole, the relationships are so damaged and so flawed, that the best option is to leave.

You might have a great relationship with your supervisor, but then you look around and see that they're a jerk to everyone else. It's possible to work in an organization where your personal experience is fine, but when you look closer you recognize that the organization itself is deeply flawed and, actually, quite awful. That's also a place you ought to get out of because it will ultimately come back and bite you. Eventually, that great supervisor *will* become a jerk to you at some point in time, so getting out is important. You only have one life to live, and you only have one world to change. Why not work for an organization where you can make a difference in the world and be happy?

Chapter 11

Build a Trusting Environment

If I have great relationships with my team members, that means I have trust. If I have trust, then when another team member, a resident, or a resident's family member comes storming in saying, "That team member did this horrible thing," I should be able to know whether there is more to the story before storming off to scream at the team member. I should know my employee well enough to consider that maybe it was an innocent misunderstanding, the resident was being unreasonable, or if the resident was mistaken. Ultimately there has to be a high level of trust. If there is trust between the team members and the leader, then people make the right decisions. You can work through almost any difficulty if you have a trusting, transformational relationship.

I recently came across a news story about an assisted living community in rural Georgia that should horrify the sensibilities of any reader. A female resident had a stroke that apparently left her close to the end of her life. The community staff called for a hospice nurse who was three hours away. The community leaders did not want to leave the woman alone so they sent three caregivers to stay with her until the nurse arrived. They were two nineteen-year-olds and a twenty-one-year-old. While very young, it is safe to assume there was some vetting and training when they were hired.

While in the resident's room they made a Snapchat video they titled *The End*. It featured obscene gestures and one of the caregivers vaping. The owner of the community found out about it when some people who saw the video reported it to the police. All three are being prosecuted for elder abuse.

I first read the story early one morning on my smartphone. I was so depressed and frustrated about this happening in the industry I love so much, that I could not figure out how to write about it. The article just sat there as an empty, open tab that was haunting me, begging to be written about, but I was at a complete loss as to how to use this as a teachable moment.

My initial reaction was to say, "Look at this, don't ever let this happen." But I knew that was not very helpful. It took me four weeks until the perfect way to use the story dawned on me. Here is what I came up with: share this story with your team and then say to them, "I am so glad you would never do this kind of thing in our community."

Discussing it this way sends all the right messages without suggesting you think they might actually do something like that. Framing it this way changes how your team looks at tempting situations so they think, "That is not the kind of person I want to be, and that is not the kind of person I am." You send the right message without ever putting them down or using your authority. You are saying in a very powerful way, I trust you.

In this "senior living sector" (we've got to decide on a better descriptor), there's all sorts of talk about millennials and baby boomers all needing, if not demanding, heightened degrees of engagement and empowerment with respect to their work, their lives, and the organizations they decide to join. Striving for, and fostering cultures that allow for these kinds of sensibilities to truly flourish is becoming ever-more important in any success we might have. The thing about this notion of "engagement and empowerment" though, is that it has to exist beyond words in a culture. At its best, a thriving culture in this field holds an actual **belief**, that by engaging and empowering *every* person across entire organizations, we actually learn more, strengthen every person, tighten every community, and allow for the discovery of what may be possible, far beyond what might be available if we were to assume that enlightenment resides only in the corner office or the board room. Increasingly, the work of leadership goes far beyond strategy and management; it takes inspired personalities who are able to rally people of all sorts together, building and invigorating community.

—Sean Kelly,
President and CEO of The Kendal Corporation

When I see people behaving the way those three caregivers in Georgia did, I first blame the caregivers, but I also find myself wondering if they had supervisors who somehow communicated to the team that they were not trustworthy, and that as a result, they lived up to that expectation. I wonder if those supervisors failed to convey that they believed their caregivers were capable of great things. I wonder if the caregivers only lived up to the low expectations they were given.

This is not to say your team won't ever disappoint you; there are always outliers. But you cannot let the outliers keep you from believing in your team. People live up to the expectations you have for them.

When I was working for Vigil Health Solutions, I called on a guy to talk about emergency call systems. I was describing one of the cool features we offered, a pocket pager for caregivers to carry so they could respond more quickly when a resident requested assistance.

The guy looked at me and exploded, "I'd never give my caregivers pagers because they would either steal or destroy them." That was enough to tell me our technology was not a fit for him, and I got out of there as fast as I could. He assumed the worst about his employees, and I am betting they delivered exactly what he expected of them. As I drove away from his office I found myself thinking, *Yeah, if I worked for you, I'd probably destroy or steal your pagers too.*

So much of creating a culture of trust comes back to this: you get from your team members what you expect from them. If I communicate to my caregivers that I know them, believe in them, and trust them, that I know they only want what is best for their residents, and that I know they are doing the very best they can, that is how they will behave.

It also means when a caregiver comes to me with a concern about a resident I am going to trust their judgment. I'm going to trust that they have a pretty good idea of what's going on with that resident and that I need to trust their intuition. The reason this works is that I really know my team down to my caregivers. I know they have a daughter in soccer and a son in little league; I know that her husband just got a great new job but that he's struggling because he drinks too much. I know all these things and I still love them for it, because I feel the best about them even though they have a messy life.

What might be my favorite story about what happens when you really trust your team members was a gift from my friend LisaAnn Shelton, an amazing senior living leader.

Bob was a memory-care resident in a senior living community that had multiple levels of care: independent living, assisted living, and memory care. One day Bob decided that he was not going to take any more showers. When his caregiver went in to help him shower Bob said, "No. I'm not gonna take a shower today."

This is hardly uncommon, so it wasn't a big deal. The caregiver responded by saying, "Okay, Bob, no problem. We'll just shower tomorrow." Almost always, the next day residents are fine with a shower. The caregiver went back the next day and Bob was still resolute. "No, I'm not going to take a shower." His refusal continued for a week. Bob would not budge.

The caregiver, of course, escalated the problem to her manager. As time went by and Bob started to smell a little ripe and it had the potential to become a real health problem, the executive director, Bob's family, and even his physician got involved. Bob was adamant. "No, I'm not taking a shower, I don't want to shower, I don't have to take a shower."

Pretty soon, every team member in the entire community knew about the "Bob problem." It got to the point where they were considering medicating him, moving him to a nursing home, or sending him to the hospital. Team members would come to work and the first thing they would ask was whether or not someone got Bob to bathe.

Over in independent living, Maria, a housekeeper, heard about what was happening with Bob. I have no idea what her inspiration was, though I wish I did, but somehow she got an idea. She had heard that Bob used to love to go dancing.

She left her housekeeping duty-station without asking permission or telling anyone what she was about to do. She went to memory care and found dirty, smelly Bob who was as stubborn as ever.

"Hi, Bob, would you like to go dancing with me?"

Bob looked at her and lit up in a way that he hadn't for years, and responded with a yes.

Then Maria asked, "If we're going to go dancing, we should get dressed up and cleaned up, right?"

Bob thought this was a good idea so Maria asked if she could help him. He was glowing at the opportunity to dance again. She got him showered and shaved. Then she went to his closet and found his old blue-pinstriped suit, a crisp, white shirt, and executive tie. Finally, she found his polished, shiny black shoes and dressed him.

He looked amazing and he felt amazing. By this time word had spread that Maria found the magic formula and there was a bit of an audience watching them. Bob looked dapper; he had a handkerchief in the breast pocket of his suit jacket. Best of all he had a huge smile on his face because he was going dancing with Maria. There was no way of knowing exactly what was going on in Bob's mind but it was like he had been transported back to his happiest moments in high school or college... at his senior prom perhaps.

Maria took Bob by the hand. They walked to the living room for memory care and she put on Bobby Darin's "Beyond the Sea." The music started and to everyone's astonishment, Bob reached out to Maria, pulled her in and led her in a marvelous, marvelous dance.

If you were there watching, even though Bob was near ninety, you could see the young man who danced and twirled young women so many decades ago. Bob's family and others watched this little miracle play out. It happened because one team member had enough of a trusting relationship with her supervisors that she could take the big risk of abandoning her post to explore an idea she had. She knew it was okay even though she worked in a completely different part of the community and was not a manager or a caregiver. Her only authorizations were an idea and a culture of trust.

Your team is like a family. Like all families, it can be healthy and functional or unhealthy and dysfunctional. We have a lot of trust in my family. I know that my wife has my back no matter what. I know that if I do something that's not right or I've made a mistake, my wife will tell me not to beat myself up because she only wants the best for me.

Even when we have our moments, I know that at her core she has my best interests at heart. That makes me feel safe. This is how great places to work function. We all want to wake up and be excited to go to work, knowing that we get to spend time with our friends doing something worthwhile.

If you have a poor company culture and your employees are miserable, you're going to have a lot of problems. The employees will tell everyone how unhappy they are with you as a leader and with your organization. This will tank your reputation. When this happens your team members become your worst enemy. They'll rob you of money, rob you of time by not working very hard, and rob you of the quality of your business by treating your customers poorly. Then those customers will tell stories about how badly they were treated or how little the staff cared.

A friend of mine sent me a video clip she received of residents in a senior living community. One woman who was ninety-years-old said, "I've only been here for sixty days and this is the third senior living community I've ever lived in, and it is the best community that I've ever lived in. The other two were terrible. They didn't treat me like a human being, they treated me like I was profit."

That woman is telling everyone how terrible those other places were. Now she's at a facility that has a positive, trusting environment and happy employees who care about their jobs and their customers. I guarantee that if you visited the facilities where the woman came from, you would discover that there is a culture problem and that the people who work at those communities do not love coming to work every day.

Disney is often held up as an example of how to create a positive culture, particularly in the area of customer service. They are a big name and it is cool to say you work for Disney or at Disneyland. But in the local southern California papers, there are a ton of stories about what it's like working for Disney. Right now, Disney is having a big fight with the city of Anaheim because the company is paying their team members so poorly that they cannot afford housing and so they sleep in their cars on the streets of Anaheim. This is a terrible thing. Who wants to work in that kind of environment? The message Disney is sending their team members is that they only care about profit, not people.

I'm suggesting we want to create the opposite of that culture. We want to create an environment where team members think, "Maybe nobody has ever heard of my company, but it is it the coolest place I have ever worked. It's the best job I have ever had." Maybe they have a chaotic home life and they are stressed about their kids, their partners, their bills, or putting food on their table. But they know that when they go to work, the people they work with will have their back.

The best result is a culture where people love coming to work every day. When this happens there is a chain reaction. If people love coming to work, they will do everything in their power to make sure they show up to work on time. Maybe they had a rough night, or they're tired, or they're just not feeling it, but they wake up in the morning and they choose to go to work because it's an environment that makes them happy and gives them purpose.

When that happy team member comes to work, they are going to work better and more efficiently. They are going to be happy with their coworkers, which makes their coworkers happy. It also means that, if a team member has a friend who is looking for work or has a job but does not like it, that team member is much more likely to recommend their workplace. And because people who are happy at work aren't looking to leave, retention is higher.

A big win with the trickle-down effect is that when your team members are happy your residents will be, too, because they can sense that everyone around them is glad to be there. If residents are happier they will feel and act more self-sufficient and demand less from team members.

The more enthusiastic your team is about working hard, the more they will create an environment where they work hard. Have you ever had this happen when going out to eat?

You sit down and, in a few minutes, your waitress takes your order for a hamburger and fries and leaves you a glass of water. After a bit, your food comes out and the waitress asks, "Do you need anything else?" You ask for some ketchup and wait for it before you start eating your food. It takes eight minutes for her to bring you the ketchup and now your food has cooled way down.

Frustrated, you realize that you finished drinking your water a long time ago and your glass has been sitting there empty. Now you are even more frustrated. You ask your waitress for more water and then you start thinking of other stuff you want. She makes multiple trips to the kitchen for you and even when you finally get everything you want, you are still frustrated.

Or, it could go something like this. Your waitress brings you water with your menu; when she comes back to take your order she refills your glass. When your food is ready, she brings it to you with ketchup for your fries and extra napkins, because she knows this particular burger is a little messy. While you're eating, she drops by with more water and the dessert menu. You're not demanding more from her because you see how great she's doing and you don't want to make her job more difficult.

This second waitress is happy with her job and takes pride in it. She made fewer trips back to the kitchen because she cares about her customers enough to anticipate their needs—she's working less because her customers are happier and she's more efficient. When you do this in the senior living environment, the residents feel the same way.

Anticipating other people's needs doesn't just happen between your team and the customers, it also happens between coworkers. That can create a dynamic environment. I am lucky to have a few incredible friendships that are based on more than common interests. One of the things that makes those friendships a delight is that those people are able to anticipate my wants, my needs, and my interests. Once or twice a year I go out to my mailbox and find a package containing a book I know I didn't order. I'll open the package and discover that my friend Dennis or my friend Denise read the book and they thought that I would love it, so they ordered a copy to be delivered to my house.

I love this, because of the meaning behind the act—they're thinking about me. What does this do to me? It makes me more careful, more thoughtful. It makes me step back and look at how I can do something for Dennis or Denise, how I could make their lives better or easier.

That's what happens in a strong, trusting relationship. When your team is happy and anticipating each other's needs, they're building up a level of trust. They know that if they make a mistake, someone will help them fix it and have their back. If they see you struggling, someone will offer to help. They go from just working alongside you and each other to actually working together. It becomes a melding of individual strengths into something beautiful that those individuals could not do alone.

Sometimes things get difficult and people make mistakes. If you have a trusting environment, your team knows that, not only do you have the organization's best interests at heart, but you have their best interests at heart. When I say to a team member, "Hey, it looks like things aren't going so great right now, let's talk about what's going on so we can make it better," it's not seen as an attack.

It's seen as a leader saying let's figure this out together because I care about you... I only want the best for you. If you are failing at something, ultimately as a leader, it's my fault. It means either I haven't given adequate direction, or I put them in the wrong place in my organization, or my organization is not a good fit for them.

If I have a problem with somebody and I don't confront it, the reason is usually because I'm trying to avoid conflict. This is a terrible thing to do to someone I care about. If your friend has spinach in their teeth, we can all agree that the right thing to do is tell them even though it might be uncomfortable. It is the same but more critical in the workplace. If I'm in a situation where one of my team members is doing something harmful to themselves or the organization, the best thing I can do is call them out. In healthy, trusting organizations, most team members will respond like this: "You're right. It's a problem and I don't know what to do about it." Now, instead of feeling that fear of conflict, you're in a position where you can help.

Everybody has strengths and weaknesses. At Senior Living Foresight, because we have a high trust level, my team can and does come to me and tell me which tasks I should delegate because I'm not good at them. We work together to create the amazing organization that is Senior Living Foresight, which is making a huge change in the senior living industry.

And yet as a team it is like we are on the Island of Misfit Toys; we would not do well in a traditional organization. We are passionate, freethinkers who can be both soft and prickly. A lot of people who work in my organization might have a tough time getting a job someplace else, starting with me. In fact, I am pretty sure if I had to find another job in the marketplace it would be nearly impossible to get someone to hire me. I am too old, I don't have a traditional resume that shows the kind of job progression or experience that would justify the kind of position I would be best suited for... and I graduated a long, long time ago from a college that at one time had the reputation for being the number one party school in the nation.

Instead, I choose to do my own thing. Rather than seeing our quirks—old, opinionated, independent, freethinker, brash—as a negative, we see them as what makes us unique and special, and we tap into that. As a leader, I ask my team things like, "What are you good at?" "What do you like doing?" "If you could do anything in this organization, what would you do?" They have the autonomy to do those things because we trust each other.

There are a few characteristics a leader must have in order to foster a trusting environment.

It's essential to have a clear vision of the thirty-thousand-foot view of what the organization is trying to accomplish. If you're a sailor who simply raises a sail and lets it blow, that vessel may not get you where you want to go. If you have an idea of the direction you want to go, you can steer your vessel so the wind is at your back. That might mean you aren't able to point your boat to sail straight there; you might have to fight the wind and you might stray a little off-course. But you still have a clear picture of the general direction you want to go.

A friend of mine works for a senior living organization whose CEO is highly respected. The CEO goes to a lot of conferences, he watches a lot of TED talks, he reads a lot of books, and he thinks about a lot of things. He wants to build a great organization and a great culture, but he has created what is ultimately an unsafe environment because he changes direction all the time. This creates a culture of distrust. He then becomes frustrated and harsh with people who don't like it. If you can't keep your organization on a path with a clear direction, you're going to have a crew that is restless.

A good leader is also flexible, open to feedback, and willing to listen. All leaders can lose direction at some point, but the difference between the CEO I was talking about in the above paragraph and a great leader is that a great leader will listen to their team members. They're willing to take criticism.

As a leader, I tend more toward the chaotic than the organized. My team has gotten used to the fact that I try things, or talk about things that never happen or that get abandoned. This sounds terrible except that they know I have a clear picture of my one goal and that is to help senior living providers do a better job.

As a result, when my employees tell me that an idea I have is not going to achieve my goal, I have to be willing to listen and change my path. You have much more of a growth mindset when you're willing to change, you're not married to your ideas, and you're open to feedback.

As I mentioned in chapter 6, Pam handles the podcast for Senior Living Foresight. She came to me the other day to discuss content for the podcast. She wanted to have some conversations with a few of the folks that we've done previous stories about in *Senior Living Foresight*. She asked me if she needed my permission or needed to go through me to talk to them. My immediate response was: "You should approach them directly." I hate seeing organizations where leadership says, "You always have to go through me." It's demeaning, it's demoralizing, and what it says is: I don't trust you.

Trust works in all directions. It needs to exist between the leadership and the people being led, and it needs to exist between all the members of the team. If someone on my team is struggling and another person helps them, there is only gratitude. No one gets defensive and no one worries that the other person is making them look badly.

We all know that we're working together to build a stronger culture and organization. Without that trust, the leaders and the team can become either a stumbling block or an auxiliary engine—you can either trip up your team or you can give them the boost they need to be successful.

Leaders must be willing to show their gratitude and appreciation. One of my long-term strategic goals is to develop relationships with major thought leaders in the broader world of business. One of those people wrote a book that I like, and was actually the target of a few *Dilbert* panels. I saw them and I thought, *Wow, that is so cool.*

I sent this person an email saying how jealous I was and what an honor it was to be targeted by Scott Adams. I received the nicest response. That author, who is a big name, needed that appreciation and affirmation. We all do. We all want to know we are valued. We want to know we are making a difference in the organization and in the lives of others.

When team members don't have a sense of being valued, they either crawl into their shells, they fight back, or they get defensive. They don't go the extra mile because that usually involves some level of risk, and why would anyone risk getting in trouble if they feel like the leader doesn't have their back?

When someone expresses gratitude and appreciation for your work, you know you're doing something right. It keeps you going, it keeps you motivated.

Leaders must also frequently talk about their mission. Sometimes I feel like I am overdoing it, but every time I have a conversation with one of my team members, I take the time to remind them that we are changing the world of senior living and that they're a big part of it. I look for as many different ways to say it as I can.

I recently received an email where the sender told me they loved what we are doing. I immediately passed it on to my team saying, "It is you and not me."

As a leader, you are ultimately the secret sauce, but at the same time, your organization would be nothing without your team. They are absolutely vital to the organization. Those team members need to know that and be reminded of that over and over again. When you share your mission, you're sending the overarching message that we are a unique, special place that's not like every place else. It is a bit like being a member of a special club.

Sometimes being a leader means being willing to make hard choices. For example, in senior living we work with families and elders that often face difficult "end-of-life choices" and often families have to make those choices for their elders. Many times they are faced with two or more terrible choices. Often there will be one choice that is less terrible than the others, but much of the time that isn't the case. It will be a bad outcome—death—either way.

When we do it right, we work with those families to help them make the best decision. We don't tell them what to do, but we help them figure out the least terrible option or the best course of action given a bunch of unhappy choices. It can be the same with your team members. Sometimes there are tough choices that need to be made and none of the options are what you would really like.

Maybe you have to lay people off, or someone is no longer a fit and you have to give them the bad news. "This is not working. I can either help you find a new job or you can take a new role within the organization." When there is no trust or low trust, that team member will be mad, stressed, and defensive. It does not have to be this way. When there is a trusting relationship in a trusting environment, that employee will recognize that you're only acting in everyone's best interest.

There is a bakery in New York, Greyston Bakery, that bakes fifty-thousand pounds of brownies every day. They have a unique hiring practice that they've trademarked: Open Hiring. Anyone who asks for a job will get one, eventually. People sign up on a list and when there's an opening, they contact the person at the top of the list to say, "Hey, you have a job."

They don't do any background checks, they don't do any drug screening, they don't look at qualifications, and they don't do any interviews. Everyone starts at minimum wage; they don't necessarily keep everyone, but everyone has a chance. Their turnover rate is incredibly low. That's a level of trust that very few organizations have achieved: the ability to trust a stranger. Imagine you've done some prison time or you're a former drug addict, and you add your name to that list. A year goes by, and you're struggling, and suddenly you get this call that says, "You have a job with us. Come on down and fill out the paperwork, no questions asked." Imagine how hard you would work for that company, because they didn't judge you and they didn't look down on you. They trusted you before even knowing you.

Who would not work very hard to honor that trust?

Last Words

I spend more time than I maybe should, thinking about what kind of an impact I will leave behind when I die. I am not sure quite why, except over the last few months I have watched as nearly a dozen friends, family members, and acquaintances passed away. In each case there was terrible pain for friends and family members. I count each one of these deaths as a loss in my life. I have also spent time thinking about the legacy each of those friends has left behind.

I am frankly struggling as I write this final section to not sound too judgmental because we all get to chart our own course and leave our own legacy. But since you have made it this far in the book I hope my thoughts will resonate. I am fearful that too often leaders don't really think about the legacy they will leave behind, yet as a leader thinking about your legacy is the most important thing you can do.

Some would argue building a big fortune, inventing a new technology, being the CEO of a company large or small are worthy life goals... worthy legacies. But I am not so sure. Others might argue that to eat, drink, and be merry is a worthy life goal. I am not sure about that, either. Actually that is not true, it is the goal of someone who has wasted their whole life.

If you have read this far, I am sure you are living for something different, something more noble, something more lasting, something bigger. Regardless of your view of God, religion, and the afterlife, we all have the unique human ability to be immortal by living a life that serves those we lead. Maybe it's not true immortality, but the way I interact with my family, my friends, and those I lead can powerfully change lives for generations to come.

At the end of the day, my dream is to be the kind of leader that will leave a legacy of powerfully making the lives of those I lead and serve better for the second, third, and fourth generations. This is also my dream for you.

Author Bio

Steve Moran is a nationally known—and sometimes controversial—writer and speaker in the senior living industry. He runs Senior Living Foresight (the new name for Senior Housing Forum), where the core value is to produce articles, videos, podcasts, and other resources that help senior living providers do a better job serving residents, team members, and the local marketplace.

Steve works with senior living communities to create better, more productive cultures. He has developed and operated large and small senior living communities, and has worked with a number of vendor companies that sell products and services to the senior living industry.

If you have a chance to hear Steve speak, be sure to ask him why he is wearing those crazy Chuck Taylor sneakers.

If you are interested in learning how to develop your coaching skills to get more from your team and grow your company culture, Steve can help you get there. For more information about keynotes, trainings, workshops, and coaching, contact **Senior Living Foresight**:

Email: smoran@seniorlivingforesight.net
Online: www.seniorlivingforesight.net

To purchase bulk copies of this book at a discount for your organization, contact **Senior Living Foresight**:

Phone: 916-390-2238

To connect with Steve Moran, you can find him via:

LinkedIn: https://www.linkedin.com/company/senior-living-forum

Facebook: https://www.facebook.com/SeniorForesight/

Instagram: https://www.instagram.com/seniorforesight/

Twitter: https://twitter.com/SeniorForesight

YouTube: https://www.youtube.com/channel/UCZ5-QZAZVkDOeVK7BI4Hg1w/

Website: https://www.seniorlivingforesight.net

Or contact him via email at: smoran@seniorlivingforesight.net.

Made in the USA
Coppell, TX
05 December 2021

67254985R00069